MEN-AT-ARMS SER[...]

EDITOR: MARTIN WIND[...]

The Venetian Empire

1200-1670

Text by DAVID NICOLLE Ph.D.

Colour plates by CHRISTOPHER ROTHERO

OSPREY PUBLISHING LONDON

Dedication
Pour Mémère.

Published in 1989 by
Osprey Publishing Ltd
59 Grosvenor Street, London W1X 9DA
© Copyright 1989 Osprey Publishing Ltd

British Library Cataloguing in Publication Data

Nicolle, David
The Venetian Empire 1200–1700.—(Men-at-arms,
210)
1. Italian military forces 1200–1700
I. Title   II. Series
355′.00945

ISBN 0-85045-899-4

Filmset in Great Britain
Printed through Bookbuilders Ltd, Hong Kong

Artist's Note
Readers may care to note that the original paintings
from which the colour plates in this book were
prepared are available for private sale. All
reproduction copyright whatsoever is retained by the
publisher. All enquiries should be addressed to:
   Scorpio Gallery
   50 High Street,
   Battle,
   Sussex TN33 0EN
The publishers regret that they can enter into no
correspondence upon this matter.

A State Apart

The story of Venice is, to some extent, separate from that of the rest of Europe. The same could be said of the city's military history and organisation. Early in the 9th century the Venetians defeated Pepin the Frank's attempts to overawe them, and they remained, at least in theory, subject to Byzantium. Gradually, however, Venice drifted into independence; and subsequently carved out its own empire at the expense of its former Byzantine masters. Their position on a series of islands set in a marshy lagoon at the head of the Adriatic made the Venetians virtually invulnerable while they steadily built up both their commercial and naval strength. In this the famous Arsenal of Venice played a leading rôle. Some kind of Byzantine-style shipyard and military depot may have existed as early as the 8th century, though the medieval Arsenal was not erected until 1104. Its name comes from the Arabic *Dar al Sina'a*, 'Dockyard', and the concept clearly owed as much to Islamic inspiration as to the Byzantine model on which the Arsenal was supposed to be based.

By 1202, and the arrival of the Fourth Crusade in Venice, the city already held much territory around the Adriatic. The menace of piracy had led Venetians to seize the pirate-infested eastern shores, where the inhabitants of many towns still spoke a form of Italian, being descended from the Latin peoples of the Roman Empire. The *Doge* or Duke of Venice already had, among his numerous titles, that of Duke of Dalmatia and Duke of Istria while the famous symbolic ceremony of *Sposalizio del Mar*, 'Marriage to the Sea', had also begun. Venetian domination of north-eastern Italy came much later; but Venice did control the lagoon coast and took a close interest in the military affairs of its neighbours, particularly in the turbulent and only partially Italian region of Friuli. Venetian merchant ventures were often almost piratical in themselves; and the city's trade contacts, stretching far beyond the Adriatic, were well established before the creation of the Crusader States led to the founding of semi-autonomous Venetian colonies on the coast of Syria and Palestine.

The military and political structure which supported these adventures in *Romania* (the Byzantine zone) and *Oltremare* (the Muslim eastern Mediterranean) was itself a mixture of East and West, Byzantine and Italian systems. These were

The *campanile* or bell-tower of Koper (Capo d'Istria) which, in the late 12th century, was Venice's main island stronghold in Istria and fell finally under Venetian rule in 1279. This 15th century tower also served as a lighthouse and observation post against pirates, such tall structures becoming symbols of Venetian sovereignty along the Yugoslav coast.

Carvings on the west door of Trogir Cathedral in Dalmatia, made by Master Radovan in 1240. Though essentially Romanesque in style, Radovan's carvings include unusual costume and weaponry reflecting the Slav population of Dalmatia. This archer (left) has a composite bow and a quiver of almost Central Asian form. The 'Guards at the Holy Sepulchre' (right) wear scale or lamellar armour over their mail hauberks and, with their wide-brimmed *chapel-de-fer* helmets, are probably based on Serbian or Byzantine soldiers.

reflected in the Doge's *Excusati* or Guard as well as his ceremonial parasol and sword. Nevertheless, the Venetian social order was strictly feudal. Though within the city no individual held land by knight tenure, various Church and other properties were tied to military service.

The Venetians were soon famous for their roving and warlike spirit, keen business acumen and pride. An almost modern sense of 'national' identity unified the city and saved Venice from many of those class struggles which rent the rest of medieval Italy. Even the *Serrate*—the 'locking' or 'closing' of the Venetian ruling class at the end of the 13th century—did not dampen the loyalty of the Venetians, rich and poor, to their Serene Republic, even though it thereafter excluded all other families from political power.

It is worth noting that only one Order of Chivalry, the *Cavalieri di San Marco*, was ever founded in Venice and no Venetian could join a foreign order without government approval. Venice remained a republic throughout its independent history, while politics and the army were kept firmly separate. Belligerent as they were, the

Venetians had a businesslike attitude to war which seems to have been regarded as an extension of commerce by other means. The early appearance of mercenaries, ancestors of the famous Italian *condottieri*, in 12th century Venice was a sign of this attitude and not of any lack of martial spirit. In fact the Venetian Republic normally tried to avoid wars, unless these were obviously going to be profitable. Nevertheless Venice suffered a very war-torn history, frequently clashing with the rival maritime republic of Genoa over the commercial domination of various regions, struggling with Hungary and later with the Ottoman Empire over Dalmatia, and being drawn into numerous wars in defence of the *Terra Firma*, Venice's mainland possessions. The *Terra Firma* was taken partly as a buffer against predatory neighbours, partly to guarantee trade routes to the Alpine passes, and partly because Venice relied on mainland wheat for its survival.

Later, of course, the Venetian Empire became locked in a life-or-death struggle with the vast Ottoman Turkish Empire. These Venetian-Ottoman wars look at first sight like a typical David and Goliath confrontation, but in military terms the Venetians were not so small as they might have appeared. From the very dawn of Venetian history all classes were called upon to fight. Venice was a great city with a population of some 200,000 by the early 15th century; was immensely wealthy, politically united, and diplomatically experienced; and had a huge navy.

The people of medieval Venice were also noted for their brawling and their love of display. While for centuries older men continued to wear traditional long dark cloaks, in the 14th century the younger men adopted tight-fitting multi-coloured hose. The designs on these leggings often indicated the *Compagnie della Calza* or 'Trouser Club' to which the wearer belonged. Sumptuary laws were constantly enacted to curb the extravagant dress of men and women, but these could lead merely to a change in fashion, as when legal but dull outer garments were slit to reveal legal but more sumptuous underclothes. This was probably the origin of 15th and 16th century 'slashed' fashions. Venetian love of display paradoxically made this maritime city a European leader when it came to jousts, tournaments and conspicuous consumption by the military élite.

In its own day Venice was seen as a paradox through its ability, as a money-minded republic, to defeat so often warlike feudal and Renaissance princes. Venice also enjoyed uncharacteristic stability despite its turbulent politics and occasional military disasters while, by the end of the 15th century, the Venetian army remained the only independent Italian military force in Italy. Even the inexorable advance of the Ottoman Turks was at first turned to advantage, Venice snapping up naval bases and colonies at a cheap price or in return for protection. In this way the Venetian Empire reached a pinnacle of power and prosperity in the mid-15th century. The cosmopolitan character of the city itself grew ever more pronounced through an obvious Dalmatian influence on many aspects of life, and the large Greek, Armenian, Muslim and black populations within Venice.

Despite Venice's maintenance of generally good relations with the Ottomans until the late 15th century, the Turkish expansion inevitably undermined Italian commercial domination of the eastern Mediterranean; and as soon as the Ottomans turned their attention to the sea a clash

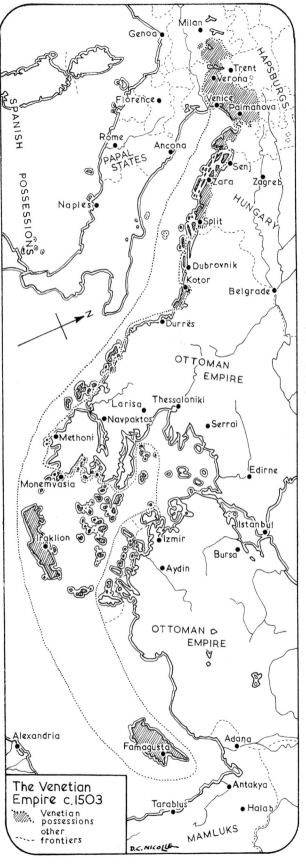

The Venetian Empire c.1503
▨ Venetian possessions
----- other frontiers

D.C. NICOLLE

became inevitable. Venice's loss of the Greek island of Evvoia in 1470 marked a turning point which was recognised even at the time. One year later the Venetians were sending armaments to Persia in a classic effort to win allies on their enemy's eastern flank. These years also saw Venice lose domination of the seas, at least beyond the Adriatic, and the start of an epic naval struggle such as had not been seen for centuries.

The Age of Expansion
1203-1509

Venice became a truly imperial power in the wake of the Fourth Crusade which, in 1204, seized the Byzantine capital of Constantinople (Istanbul) and, with Venetian aid, temporarily established a 'Latin Empire' in the Byzantine heartland. The success of many such Western military ventures into the eastern Mediterranean depended upon an ability to transport war-horses long distances by sea. This problem had apparently been solved by the Venetians in the 12th century with their use of larger ships and a system of carrying adequate drinking water.

The Fleet

Venice's power depended, of course, upon its fleets which, whether peaceful or warlike, were commanded by an admiral advised by two government-appointed civilians. Beneath the admiral were *proveditori*, administrators and *sopracomiti*, galley captains. The chain of command was tightened as the centuries passed, but galley captains always had a tendency to act as free agents, despite the creation of a Captain General of the Sea in overall naval command. A system of naval patrols was also set up in the 13th century to control the most sensitive seas and, where possible, to cut off enemy supplies.

The limitations of medieval shipping meant that Venice could never entirely control any part of the Mediterranean, though Venetian trade could be protected and piracy suppressed. A convoy system was nothing new, but by the 13th century escorts of from 15 to 30 galleys protected many slow and vulnerable merchant 'round ships'. These convoys, their routes and destinations, were strictly regulated by the government, but if their escorting galleys could be lured away or defeated, then Venetian losses could be crippling. Such convoys were, however, only seen in dangerous seas or in wartime as, for example, when Venice was locked in one of her numerous conflicts with her arch-rival, Genoa. The very limited operational range of medieval galleys at first confined convoy escorts to the chain of naval bases which constituted the Venetian overseas empire, or to friendly ports. Only the building of much larger merchant-galleys, which were able to defend themselves, enabled this convoy system to be extended beyond the Mediterranean, out into the Atlantic and even to the coasts of England and Flanders. The absence of a Venetian galley fleet could also influence events on land, as when the Byzantines took advantage of such a situation to recapture Istanbul from the 'Latin Empire' in 1261. Furthermore, galleys had to defend their own bases, captains and crews manning the walls whenever they were attacked by land.

Over 3,000 Venetian merchant ships were trading by the mid-15th century, and many of these could be readily converted into warships or at least into military transports. In the Arsenal were a reserve of originally 25, later 50 and eventually 100 war-galleys. The defensive equipment carried by each ship was closely regulated by the government. In 1255 a small vessel carried five assorted crossbows, a large ship at least eight, plus helmets,

The port of Amasra on the Black Sea, though held by Venice's deadly rival Genoa, was a typical Italian medieval fortified outpost surrounded by potentially hostile territory and existing solely to secure the home city's trading network. Amasra finally fell to the Ottomans in 1460.

shields, javelins, spears and grappling hooks. Medieval ships also had very large crews, particularly when 'armed' for a voyage in dangerous waters.

Even a merchant ship would then carry at least 60 men, an ordinary galley from 240 to 280. Skilled sailors were recruited in Venice, Dalmatia and Greece. There were no galley-slaves in the Middle Ages and oarsmen came from Venice or its empire, particularly from Dalmatia. Venetian oarsmen were selected by lot from the city's parishes, being financially supported by those who remained behind. From the 14th century debtors were recorded working off their obligations at the oars. Rowing skills were encouraged through races and regattas in Venice, especially on the feast day of St Paul. Other competitions included a sort of rough water polo, and water-tilting: here jousters stood on the stern of each boat as they rowed towards each other, the loser being pushed into the canal. At sea sailors and oarsmen were armed with swords or spears, but changes in weapons technology gradually led to a decline in the military status of the ordinary sailor. Yet all aboard were still expected to fight when necessary, even the merchant passengers. Every man had his weapon, the most important being stored beneath the captain's cabin.

Professional soldiers or marines had always sailed aboard ship, but their rôle became more important as weaponry became more powerful and expensive. Venetians used javelins as late as the 15th century, while other weapons included cooking pots filled

The fortified galley-harbour at Amasra where Genoese ships could shelter, not only from the Black Sea's fearsome storms but also from rival Venetian, Ottoman and other fleets. It was a very simple structure compared to the later Venetian galley-harbour at Zadar (see page 24).

Carved ivory cantle of an early 14th century Italian saddle. Here a knight has a great helm and early forms of plate armour for his arms and legs (Louvre, Paris).

with soap to make the enemy's decks slippery, fire-grenades and blinding sulphur. Swimmers could even attack the foe's hull, threatening to sink him—though in fact very few ships were actually sunk in medieval warfare. Crossbows were now the main long-distance weapon, contact and boarding still deciding the final outcome. In 1303 the government instructed that each galley carry 30 such crossbowmen, who would also row on the inner benches. Shooting practice was compulsory in Venice, citizens training at the butts in groups of 12. They also competed in three annual competitions where the government offered rich prizes: valuable scarlet cloth for the winner, a shorter length of cloth plus a new crossbow and quiver for the runners up. One group of crossbowmen known as the 'noble bowmen' were recruited from the aristocracy and served aboard both war galleys and armed merchantmen from the late 14th century onwards, having the privilege of living in the captain's cabin. Such service could also be the first step in a military or political career. Few professional mercenaries yet seem to have served at sea, and no maritime *condottieri* are recorded until the mid-16th century.

Another important foundation of Venetian might was her ability to mass-produce ships in the Arsenal. These now had the frame-first system which differed from Graeco-Roman shipping in that the ribs or frame were constructed before the planking was applied, the ancients having made a planked hull to which they then attached the ribs. This modern system was not only faster but used much less wood. War-galleys were themselves also changing. Though the differences between early

Carved capitals on the lowest level of the Doge's Palace, Venice, early 14th century. Among the military figures on these carvings are a head wearing a bascinet and mail aventail with loosened bretache hanging from the chin (left); and a fully armoured rider carrying an unidentified weapon (right).

medieval Byzantine *dromons*, with their two banks of oars, and the single-banked Italian war-galley are not yet entirely clear, a new system of grouping the oars does seem to have been invented in the 11th or 12th centuries. This system *alla sensile*, or 'in simple fashion', was itself to be superceded early in the 16th century. 'Great galleys', designed specifically for long-distance trade in dangerous waters, also appeared in the mid-14th century. Heavily defended, though bulky and unwieldy, merchant 'round ships' also proved their worth against the Ottomans when the latter suddenly turned to naval warfare late in the 15th century. By then Mediterranean ships employed the more efficient stern rudder instead of the steering oars that had been used since antiquity. Though this invention is generally believed to have entered the Mediterranean from northern Europe, recent evidence shows that it was known to Muslim mariners as early as the 11th century and may also have been known to the Byzantines. Other technical advances included the compass, which was clearly of Islamic and ultimately Chinese origin.

Ramming was no longer an important naval tactic, the true ram having been replaced by the higher and more flimsy *calcar* or boarding 'beak' early in the Middle Ages; but even a *calcar* could smash the enemy's oars and cripple his rowers. A galley's defences were concentrated in the bow, where a stone-throwing catapult might also be mounted in the wooden *rembata* or castle, and to a lesser extent in the stern. Wooden parapets or *impavesati* ran along each side of the ship to protect the oarsmen. Greek Fire and other pyrotechnics were greatly feared, some ships being swathed in protective vinegar-soaked hides or sheets of felt in time of battle. Yet battles on the open sea remained rare. Apart from defending convoys and suppressing piracy, the primary function of the Venetian galleys seems to have been in 'combined operations', supporting a landing force either to attack an enemy base or defend their own. The Venetians were noted experts when it came to attacking harbours and sea walls. Even the catapult aboard ship was, in fact, called a *litaboli* or 'shore buster'. Wooden towers could be erected on deck to overtop the land defences. Small boats could be slung between the mast-heads to carry crossbowmen, and spars could be swung from ropes as battering rams.

When battle between opposing fleets did occur it often began with the same ceremonious courtesy as a land battle. A special flag, with a sword pointing skywards, could be raised to signal a willingness to fight, and enemy standards would be trailed in the water behind victorious ships when they returned to port. A commander's primary tactical consideration was to keep his fleet together. Then he had to make best use both of his low but fast and manoeuvrable galleys and his slow but tall and almost invulnerable 'round ships'. Above all he had to break the enemy formation before overwhelming it piecemeal by boarding. This could be achieved by feigning flight, then turning on the foe; or by catching his galleys with their sails up and oars stowed. Navigation was almost always within sight of land, so that a concealed part of the fleet could launch an ambush from behind islands, capes or bays. Consequently small scouting vessels also had a vital rôle to play in naval warfare. If necessary warships could be lashed together to form a static floating fortress. They could be beached with their strongly defended bows pointing out to sea, or be moored stern to the beach ready to be cut loose at a moment's notice.

Even the appearance of the first cannon aboard ship did little to change such traditional tactics until the late 16th century. Such *bombards* were recorded in the forecastles of a few Venetian galleys in the 1370s, and became standard armament in the 15th century. Numerous small guns were by then mounted on galleys and round ships to cut down the enemy crew, while a single larger cannon could be placed in a galley's bow to pierce the enemy's hull or topple his mast. Such weaponry at first proved very successful against Ottoman galleys, whose crews still mostly used composite bows.

River Warfare

Venice was also involved in warfare along the broad rivers, lakes and marshes of northern Italy, though not always with great success. Most such campaigns arose after Venice conquered wide territories on the *Terra Firma* in what are now Lombardy, the Veneto and Friuli, where river fleets could support Venetian land armies. Full-sized galleys operated on Lake Garda and great rivers like the Po. Reference to the first *galleons* probably meant small galleys with an upper fighting deck over the oarsmen. Other vessels included sailing ships, and the little *barche* which carried only three rowers and two crossbowmen. Venice maintained sizeable fleets of such vessels until the use of accurate cannon, firing from a river's banks, put an effective end to this type of warfare at the end of the 15th century. This was, however, a form of combat in which some of Venice's rivals were already skilled. Even the fleet of six galleys and 25 smaller craft which Venice launched on Lake Garda in the winter of 1439–40 was almost immediately destroyed by Milanese lake craft. This had been an epic of military engineering in which, for 15 days, the Venetians hauled their ships up the River Adige and across a low mountain range to Lake Garda.

The castle at Trogir, Dalmatia, which still has carved Venetian coats-of-arms set into its walls.

The Army

The Venetian army was quite as effective as its fleet, despite jibes that the marsh-dwelling Venetians didn't know how to ride properly. The armies of 13th century Italian states already included mercenaries from other parts of the country in addition to a feudal leader's own *masnada*. Most early 13th century Venetian troops were, however, still recruited from the lagoon area, plus a few Dalmatian and Istrian feudal contingents. In emergencies, like that of 1294, the Venetian parishes registered all males between 17 and 60 years of age and listed all the weapons they possessed, those called to fight being organised into groups of 12. Such domestic troops, conscripts and volunteers, were still preferred to mercenaries in 14th century Venice. Most fought on foot while richer men or aristocrats served as a cavalry, as they did in all Italian cities. A register of 1338 estimated that 30,000 Venetians could bear arms; nor were they a mere rabble, as in some other medieval urban militias. Many were skilled crossbowmen, while others fought with slings and fire-grenades. Venice also had its own local professional soldiers, a small corps of infantry guarding vital castles like Mestre and Treviso; but no full-time Venetian cavalry were as yet recorded in the 14th century.

The first true Venetian standing army emerged quite suddenly early in the 15th century and consisted, as elsewhere in Italy, of *condottieri* mercenary contract soldiers. Such a force was clearly needed to defend Venice's new mainland territories on the *Terra Firma*. The Republic's contribution to an alliance with Florence in 1426

Effigy of unnamed Venetian knight, mid/late 14th century. The man wears typical armour of his period, though the crossing of the chains from his coat-of-plates to his sword and dagger, and the large buckle-cover on his sword-belt, seem to have been fashionable in Venice. (Victoria & Albert Mus., London)

consisted of no less than 8,000 cavalry and 3,000 infantry in time of war, 3,000 and 1,000 respectively in peacetime. The almost continuous warfare of the first half of the 15th century led to such standing armies, their support systems and associated taxation becoming an accepted fact of Venetian life, while the mainland city of Brescia became the *de facto* headquarters of the Venetian army. Uniforms were at first rare and only ceremonial, being emblazoned with the Lion of St Mark. Later in the 15th century red and white striped jerkins for at least the *provisionati di S. Marco* militia became increasingly common. Rewards for loyalty or success included generous cash payments even to the humble rank-and-file, pensions for the wounded or bereaved and honours for their leaders. This was clearly no longer a medieval army, but a Renaissance force with many modern attributes and attitudes.

Venetian tactics on land were the same as those of other Italian armies[1]. In the 12th and 13th centuries militia infantry fought in close-packed ranks with large shields and used their spears as pikes, though there was already an increasing number of crossbowmen protected by similarly large shields. High standards of disciplines and close co-operation between horse and foot also set such Italian forces apart from those of the rest of Europe. Fourteenth century Venetian armies had to face Hungarian invasions in Friuli as well as the forces of other Italian cities. On occasion Venetian armoured cavalry dismounted to fight defensively on foot in what was then regarded as an English tactic. When the lagoon itself was invaded by Genoese and Paduan forces in 1379 the Venetians built wooden

[1]See Men-at-Arms 136, *Italian Medieval Armies 1300–1500*.

forts and palisades, barricaded some canals with chained ships, blocked others with sunken barges, and harassed the enemy in both small boats and galleys. Venice not only survived this threat but triumphed, and went on to win extensive *Terra Firma* territories in 1404–5.

From then until the crisis of 1509 Venetian land forces were generally on the offensive and proved to be the most effective in Italy. They fought not only Italians and Hungarians but also Germans and French longbowmen who, in 1449, used English archery tactics against Venice's great *condottiere* leader Bartolomeo Colleoni. Just under 30 years later the Venetians were faced with full-blown Ottoman Turkish raids deep into Friuli. This was something totally new and, despite Venetian experience of war against Muslim Turks in their overseas empire, the defences of Friuli failed dismally. The Venetians had to withdraw into their fortresses, leaving the countryside to the faster lightly equipped Ottoman cavalry. The one major battle resulted in a serious Venetian defeat, although, by assembling a much larger army, the Venetians did beat off later Ottoman raids. Such experiences convinced Venice to employ its own *stradioti* 'colonial' light cavalry on Italian soil, to improve its domestic military training, and to overhaul the system of selective conscription. However, another series of Ottoman raids in 1499 again proved to be virtually unstoppable. A massive French invasion of Italy at the end of the 15th century brought a series of devastating defeats for the Venetian army, culminating in the disasters of 1509. Yet even in 1508 the Venetians had managed to beat off a determined invasion by the Emperor Maximilian of Germany: not only was his army defeated in the mountains near Pieve di Cadore, but Venice counter-attacked and captured further territory in Friuli and Istria.

Command of the army differed from that of the

fleet. An ancient tradition stated that Venetian noblemen could command detachments of no more than 25 men, yet an overall Master of Soldiers had been known since the earliest days. The position of Captain General appeared as an emergency measure in the 14th century, but overall management of military affairs still lay with a civilian committee of 20 *Savii* or Wise Men. Remarkable as it might seem, such constant civilian and political interference in military and naval affairs did not affect efficiency; in fact it saved Venice from the military take-overs which plagued other Italian city-states. Long experience of seafaring and naval warfare gave Venice a supply of men well able to accept the responsibilities of leadership, particularly of infantry forces. Armies were normally commanded by Venetian noblemen, though professionals from the *Terra Firma* and later even mercenary *condottieri* were given command. Venetian military thinking was, however, singularly cautious. Lust for glory ran a poor second to achieving victory with the minimum expenditure of both blood and treasure. Another feature of Venetian military life was the *proveditore* or civilian commissioner, who accompanied an army and kept a watchful commissar-like eye on everything, particularly on the mercenaries. A series of new *proveditori* rôles was set up in the late 15th century, including the combat rank of commanding ferocious Balkan or Greek *stradioti* forces in Italy. By 1509 these supposedly civilian commissioners also commanded the Italian light cavalry and the artillery.

Cavalry

Despite their web-footed reputation, the Venetians had fielded effective armoured cavalry even in the

Mid-15th century carving of unknown Venetian coat-of-arms supported by two soldiers in distinctive Venetian colonial armour. On the left, a fully equipped man-at-arms wears a helmet remarkably similar to some found in the Venetian fortress at Khalkis (see line-drawings). On the right a similarly armoured crossbowman spans his weapon using a cranequin or rack-and-pinion system (*in situ* Jurja Barakovica Street, Sibenik).

13th century, a regulation of 1239 assuming one war-horse, two other horses and three squires for each Venetian knight. The 14th century poet Petrarch declared that this 'nation of sailors' surpassed all others both on horseback and at sea. Various Venetian aristocrats bred fine horses on their mainland estates, though most animals were imported from Germany and Hungary. The war-horse was by far the most expensive part of a man-at-arm's equipment. By the 15th century it became normal to attack an enemy's animal rather than the rider, thus making losses higher and the problems of replacement even worse.

Heavy cavalry were organised into small units of *lanze*—this consisting of a man-at-arms, a lightly armed sergeant and a page or mounted servant. By the 15th century many if not most such men-at-arms were short-term *condottieri* mercenaries. A more stable formation, the *lanze spezzate* or 'broken lance', was meanwhile established, consisting of veteran or picked troops permanently committed to

Effigy of Federico Cavalli, late 14th century. The Cavalli were a military family, some of whom served Venice as *condottieri* mercenaries (*in situ* church of S. Anastasia, Verona).

Canal entrance to the Arsenal, Venice, looking towards the site of the Old Arsenal. The Gate of the Arsenal, on the left, was rebuilt in monumental style in 1572 following victory over the Ottoman fleet at Lepanto.

Venetian service. The man-at-arm's equipment was now so expensive that a separation began to appear between the fully armoured *elmetti* and the slightly less prestigious *utili*. Numerous severe defeats suffered by armoured cavalry at the hands of infantry during the 14th century had clearly not undermined faith in the man-at-arm's military potential. His armour was now so sophisticated that the *lanze* enjoyed a renewed lease of life well into the 16th century. Fifteenth century Venetian *lanzi* also included mounted crossbowmen and even mounted hand-gunners, though not the infantry component that appeared in France and Burgundy. Along with the employment of *stradioti*, Venetian forces now recruited a variety of other types of separate and more mobile light cavalry formations. In fact, Venice played a leading rôle in the development of western European light cavalry during the late medieval and Renaissance periods.

Infantry

Given the ancient Venetian tradition of all classes carrying arms and of the government encouraging military training among the ordinary people, it is not surprising to find that Venetian infantry were both numerous and effective. Among the earliest were the Militias of the Six Wards or districts of Venice. In 1262 these *sestieri* were increased to 500 men per parish, partly to help the *Signori di Notti* maintain order at night. In the 14th century these men were still selected by lot. Men chosen for the prestigious and lucrative rôle of crossbowmen aboard merchant ships and galleys were also selected from among the best at the various shooting ranges in Venice. Men aged between 15 and 35 were enrolled as crossbowmen by their parish, then being divided into *duodene* (groups of 12) under a local officer who was also responsible for their training at the local butts. Since all classes lived crowded together within Venice, the *duodene* included rich and poor, noble and commoner, who trained and fought together. Not all fought as crossbowmen, of course. Other infantry weapons designed specifically to combat cavalry included the long mace-like weapons and barbed spears which wrought havoc among invading Hungarians in 1373.

The élite of Venetian infantry were, however, drawn from the ranks of the *Arsenalotti*, the highly skilled and well-paid craftsmen of the Arsenal. They provided guards for the Doge's Palace and other government buildings, acting as a police force and even a fire-brigade, as well as furnishing detachments of well-equipped infantry. The Arsenal itself was also a weapons factory and arms store, as well as being the most famous ship-building yard in Europe. In 1314 no less than 1,131 crossbows were stored within its walls, while its new rope-making factory, dating from 1303, made thousands of crossbow-strings. The *Compagni della Calza* or 'Trouser Clubs', which had been created in the 15th century largely for the entertainment of the young men, also provided trained volunteers when called upon, while the unemployed could also find themselves enlisted. In real emergencies Venice fell back upon mass conscription so that Venetian infantry forces could sometimes be very large—up to 20,000 at the start of the 16th century.

By this time militia officers wore a breastplate and a sallet helmet, but the quality of their troops varied considerably. In general Venetian militia remained by far the best in Italy, though those of Venice itself were normally superior to those of the *Terra Firma*. In fact the latter were often used merely as pioneers or labourers. The status of infantry had sunk considerably by the year 1500, despite the appearance of Italian hand-gunners in the 1440s and the division of infantry formations into 'assault' troops with swords or short spears, and 'fire' companies with crossbows or guns. In 1490 efforts had been made to train two men from each *Terra Firma* village with handguns but not until the crisis of 1509 had passed could a full overhaul of the Venetian militia system be carried out.

Armies at home and abroad

Venice's first serious involvement on the *Terra Firma* dated from 1338, with her defeat of Padua and seizure of Treviso. Henceforth Venice was a major power on the Italian mainland, and after 1423 a fundamental shift in Venetian policy committed her to further territorial expansion. Venice went on to conquer a large part of northern and north-eastern Italy. Though the government and military organisation of these territories varied, it was generally less oppressive than elsewhere in Italy. Venice was, of course, primarily concerned with security, food supplies and access to the Alpine passes rather than military glory, so that her light hand inspired considerable loyalty on the *Terra Firma*. This was even true in a backward and still essentially feudal area like Friuli, where the warlike Friulani were noted as swordsmen. *Terra Firma* urban militias or *Ordinanze* trained each Sunday,

Statue of 'Orlando' by Bonino of Milan, 1413. This knight, representing Dubrovnik, wears typical early 15th century Italian armour of the kind used by the military élite of Dalmatia (*in situ* main square, Dubrovnik).

'St Michael', wall painting by Vincent of Kastav, 1474. Part of a cycle of paintings in Istria which include typically Venetian weapons such as the three-bladed *ronco* and, as here, typical German armour. Venetian Istria was bounded by Austria while Hungary and Ottoman-ruled Bosnia lay just over the mountains (*in situ* church of St. Mary, Beram).

Istanbul (Constantinople) in 1204, Venice carefully selected a number of strategic territories as her share of the shattered Byzantine Empire. She was not interested in large mainland territories which would be difficult to defend and expensive to govern. Rather the Venetians wanted domination of the lucrative trade routes, so they took part of Istanbul itself, a chain of islands and most of the best harbours around Greece. Finally they bought the great island of Crete for 30 lbs of gold. Venice had thus, at one stroke, won an empire. Organising it was another matter. The old Venetian territories in the Adriatic had retained their traditional systems of government, though under Venetian counts or local families of proven loyalty. The new empire in 'Romania', as it was known, was placed under governors sent directly from Venice. Crete was slightly different on account of its size; a Venetian duke was responsible for the island's defences and presided over a new feudal class of colonists, plus those few Greek aristocrats who retained their land.

Permanent military forces soon appeared elsewhere in this empire, long before they did in the *Terra Firma*. Most were enlisted from the local and totalled about 30,000 men. In many areas the old country levies had remained effective fighting troops throughout the 13th century. Such forces were revived early in the 16th century when they were known as *cernide*. Elsewhere the peasantry served as rural guerrillas, harassing an invader. On the other hand the full-time urban garrisons of the Venetian *Terra Firma* were often of very low quality, consisting of retired veterans or men with no military training whatsoever.

Venetian forces stationed overseas in the empire 'Da Mare', were of more consistent quality and often occupied isolated or hazardous outposts. Apart from the huge booty won with the conquest of

Rear view of Verrocchio's statue (*c.*1485) of the famous *condottiere* Bartolomeo Colleoni who served Venice faithfully for many years. It shows a perfect example of late 15th century full-plate armour in the Italian style. For a front view see MAA 136, *Italian Medieval Armies* p.34 (*in situ* Campo SS. Giovanni e Paolo, Venice).

'Battle of Anghiari (1440)', painted *cassone* chest by school of Uccello. In this battle the Venetians and Florentines under Sforza defeated the Milanese under Piccinino. (Nat. Gall. of Ireland, Dublin)

military élites, though even in the 13th century Italians were being recruited for service overseas. In 1369 Venice's Cretan feudatories rose in revolt. The rising was crushed after bitter fighting, and thereafter the defences of Crete were stiffened by many mercenaries, Italian infantry taking a major rôle though Italian cavalry were more rarely recorded. Local *stradioti* provided the bulk of horse-soldiers.

Each part of the Venetian empire differed in the details of its military organisation. Istria had finally been conquered late in the 13th century after a series of amphibious operations by galley fleets. The fortifications of those places, like Trieste and Koper which had defied Venetian control, were dismantled. Koper was placed under the joint rule of a *podesta* civil governor and a *proveditore* military administrator. Zadar, the main Venetian naval base in Dalmatia, frequently revolted against Venetian rule and had, in fact, been recovered during the first battle of the Fourth Crusade. Dubrovnik resisted Venetian control more effectively and was only ruled by Venice from 1205 to 1358. Elsewhere the Venetians left day-to-day

affairs in local hands while firmly controlling the ports, those islands with a tradition of piracy, and access to the vital forests from which most Venetian ships were built. Otherwise Venice had no interest in the bleak limestone mountains of the hinterland. Some cities were obliged to supply ships to the Venetian fleet—Zadar no less than 30 galleys fully manned—while all had to supply sailors, plus militias for their own defence. Though the countryside remained firmly Slav, the Italian character of the major Dalmatian cities was strengthened. Fully trained crossbow militias became a feature of these cities, while Dalmatian peasant warriors still apparently used composite bows of Byzantine or almost Turkish form.

The Middle Eastern character of Venetian colonial troops in Crete and Greece was even more obvious. Evvoia, known to the Venetians as Negroponte, was almost as big an island as Crete and was the key to Venetian power in the Aegean.

It bristled with fortifications, including a tower built in the midst of the Euripos channel where up to 14 tides flowed in a single day. Only one of the most senior Venetian administrators could become *Bailie* or governor of Evvoia, and the colony's own flag was flown on a bronze flag-staff outside the Cathedral of San Marco in Venice itself on ceremonial occasions.

Other less important Aegean islands were mere stops along the trade routes or bases from which to control piracy. The Cyclades archipelago, theoretically a fief of the Latin Empire of Constantinople, was actually held by various Venetian families who placed loyalty to Venice above mere feudal obligations to that short-lived 'empire'. The tiny island of Kithera, off the southern tip of Greece, provided vital communications between Venice and Crete; it eventually had no less than three castles and a sizeable garrison. Corfu, at the mouth of the Adriatic, had originally fallen to Venice during the carving-up of the Byzantine Empire, its feudal obligation being the supply of 20 knights and 40 squires. Corfu was, however, soon lost to the Kingdom of Naples and had to be purchased back in 1386. Other temporary Venetian possessions in Greece included Monemvasia, Methoni, Argos, Corinth, Navpaktos, Nauphlia and even Athens.

As the Ottomans advanced across Greece in the 14th century these outposts became filled with Byzantine refugees. Many came from the old military élite and took service with Venice as *stradioti* light cavalry. Among them were famous names like Graitzas Palaeologos, from the last Byzantine ruling family, who rose to command all Venetian light cavalry. An effort to drive the Ottomans out of the Peloponnese in 1463–4 with an army of *stradioti*, Italian hand-gunners and *condottieri* heavy cavalry failed. This was the last major Venetian land offensive in the east. Thereafter defensive operations were left to the naval and garrison infantry and to *stradioti*, who not only fought the Ottomans on their own terms but were much cheaper to maintain than Western-style men-

'Venetian *Stradiotti* at the battle of Fornovo (1495)' from a French print made a few years later. Here a combined Italian army under Venetian leadership was narrowly defeated by the invading French, but not before the *stradiotti* light cavalry had caused terror on the French flank. (Nat. Gall. of Art, Washington)

at-arms. Wielding short lances or javelins, bows and light swords, and being relatively lightly armoured, such *stradioti* were recruited in Greece, Albania and Dalmatia. Their loyalty was rarely in doubt, their ferocity proverbial, and their habit of collecting the heads of slain foes never seriously discouraged. Nevertheless, signs of declining Balkan and Greek support for Venice became apparent even by the 15th century.

Crete remained the prize possession and Venice had to fight for it against both local Greeks and Genoese free-booters. To ensure its subjection the island had been divided into six sections named after the six districts of Venice. Beneath these came 132 knights' fees and 405 infantry sergeantries mostly held by Venetian military settlers. Fortifications sprang up all over the island, particularly along the northern coast. Yet Crete proved not to be the land of opportunity as had at first been hoped. Even by 1332 many of the Venetian settler knights were too poor to afford proper military equipment. Many of their feudal serfs were of Arab origin, descended from Muslim conquerors who had ruled Crete centuries earlier. Though unfree, they could be summoned for military service, while Greek Cretans were also conscripted when needed. The Cretan talent for savage guerrilla warfare first became apparent during the mid-13th century rebellion which was, however, equally savagely crushed. Another uprising in the mid-14th century confirmed the Venetians in their view of Cretans as untrustworthy savages, and the latter in their hatred for Venetian colonial rule. Nevertheless Cretan infantry archers were soon fighting alongside Venetian crossbowmen in the *Terra Firma*.

From the Fourth Crusade's conquest of Istanbul in 1204 to the Byzantine regaining of their capital in 1261, Venetian merchants dominated the Black Sea. This dangerous area spanned the rich caravan routes from Iran and China, and was also an important source of wood from which crossbows were made. In 1261 Venice lost her paramount position to the Genoese, who were close allies of a revived Byzantium. But, despite the dedicated hostility of these two Italian maritime republics, Venice and Genoa frequently co-operated in the hazardous environment of the Black Sea. This was particularly apparent in the Crimea, where a number of originally Byzantine ports served as

'Portrait of an unknown Florentine knight' by Piero di Cosimo, *c*.1515, showing the fluted armour popular in northern Italy from the early 16th century. (Nat. Gallery, London)

termini for the trans-Asian Silk Road as well as routes north into fur-rich Russia and Siberia. There were, of course, bloody clashes, but Venetians and Genoese both feared the might of the neighbouring Mongol Golden Horde and its successor Khanates. The Crimea itself was a remarkably mixed area, with Armenians forming a majority in some trading towns and Christian Goths, descendants of Dark Age and perhaps subsequent Anglo-Saxon refugee settlers, inhabiting the coastal mountains. At Kaffa the Genoese even had a *capitaneus Gothie* in charge of Gothic troops, plus *castellani* and other full-time military officials. The Italians lost the Crimea to the Ottomans in 1479, the Black Sea becoming an Ottoman lake within five years, after which the only 'Western' merchant vessels to sail its waters were those of Venice's old Dalmatian rival, Dubrovnik.

The mercenary element in Venetian armies steadily increased over the centuries. Mercenaries had long been a feature of Italian warfare and northern Italy remained the major source of such

'Knight adoring the Virgin and Child' by Catena, early 16th century. The warrior's turban and a curved dagger on the wall suggest that he represents an 'oriental', perhaps one of the Three Wise Men or a Venetian *stradiot* light cavalryman. (Nat. Gallery, London)

troops for Venice. Among the first non-Italians to be hired were Catalan crossbowmen late in the 13th century. Foreigners became more common in 14th century Venice, as they were elsewhere in Italy, though the Venetians earned a reputation as notably hard bargainers when it came to drawing up the *condotta* contract. Such contracts were generally very detailed, specifying arms and equipment down to the last detail. Foreign mercenaries were not normally permitted to live in Venice itself but were housed in barracks or bachelor houses within the citadels of the *Terra Firma*. There the troops soon integrated into the local communities, marrying local girls and even setting up local businesses. Yet discipline could still be harsh, with hangings or mutilations for serious offenses like desertion. *Condottieri* leaders who betrayed Venice were publicly humiliated by having their portraits hung upside-down in public places such as the Rialto brothel.

Condottieri infantry were sent overseas in the 14th century, serving in Crete and elsewhere. The greatest successes of these highly trained professionals were, however, in defence of the *Terra Firma*. These were achieved not only against other *condottieri* but most notably against Hungarians in Friuli early in the 15th century. Among Venice's non-Italian mercenaries were German gunners and pikemen, English archers, Gascons, Swiss, Albanian mountain infantry, Dalmatians and Cretan archers. *Condottieri* infantry were used in great numbers during the 15th century, proving much easier to hire and fire than the prouder and more expensive cavalry. Such mercenary infantry forces normally included spearmen, crossbowmen and shield-bearers in equal number. But all these mercenary forces had the disadvantage of short contracts, after which the men could go and hire out to another state.

The long Venetian tradition of military training and splendid tournaments, in which even *stradioti* were taking part by 1491, stood Venice in good stead. Archery butts for crossbow practice were dotted around the city and the Lido. Prizes were generous, and in 1506 shooting ranges and competitions for handguns were similarly set up, indicating just how important these new weapons had become. Other warlike pastimes included barely controlled battles with staves and fists between the three eastern and the three western *sestieri* parishes of Venice. Officially inaugurated in 1292, they tended to take place between September and Christmas. Normally focusing on the bridges—which lacked parapets in those days—they ended with the losers falling into the canal. Sham sea fights, assaults on mock castles, and *bagordi* or light cavalry manoeuvres of attack and withdrawal clearly inspired by Balkan or Islamic military practice, were also a feature of 15th century Venice. So was the clearly non-European *Moresca* war dance with blunted daggers. On a more serious level twice-yearly military parades and inspections were designed to weed out incompetent troops and to check the quality of military equipment.

Siege, Fortification and Firearms

Venetian siege warfare, at least on land, followed the same patterns as elsewhere in Europe. By the early 16th century the defence of a city like Padua depended upon an exterior water-filled ditch and massed artillery in raised earth bastions to cover gates and other weak points. The stone city wall was strengthened by having earth piled against its inner face behind which was another ditch backed by casemates and towers. Finally there came a high embankment with a parapet serving as an assembly point and additional artillery platform. Crossbows were still used by militiamen, but handgunners provided the most effective answer to infantry assault.

Venice first used, and faced, firearms in 1376 when both the Venetians and Austrians employed bombards in open battle. Guns played a more significant rôle against the Genoese a few years later; and by the early 15th century the Venetian army clearly had an artillery train while even the river fleets carried numerous small cannon.

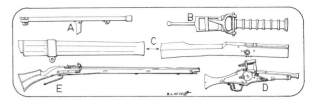

Firearms: *A*—Barrel of *Schioppo* hand-gun, 14th C. (Mus. Civico Marzoli, Brescia); *B*—Breech-loading cannon seen from beneath, of type which could be mounted on the bulwarks of a ship, 15th C. (Mus. Civico Marzoli, Brescia); *C*—Mid-15th C. handgun, shown on right in reconstructed wooden stock (Mus. Civico, Trieste); *D*—Military wheellock pistol with German barrel & Brescian stock, mid-16th C. (Armoury of Doge's Palace, Venice); *E*—Italian caliver matchlock, length almost 1.5 metres (after Held).

Grenades were also recorded, but it was the development of the hand-gun which was to prove most dramatic. In the 14th century such weapons had less armour-penetrating capability than crossbows, though they were cheaper; but improvements in the manufacture of saltpetre and the use of longer barrels rapidly increased muzzle velocity. The great Venetian *condottiere* leader, Colleoni, was popularly credited with first using field artillery on mobile carriages, and though he might not actually have been the first, he certainly used these new weapons very effectively. The Venetians were also enthusiastic about developing new explosive weapons, including gunpowder-filled mines and the long-barrelled and highly mobile *basilisk* siege gun. The Arsenal obviously played a major part in these developments, but was equally clearly unable to manufacture as many cannon as were needed in the 15th century. Meanwhile iron was smelted and worked for military purposes in a walled area of furnaces known as the Getto, later to become better known as the Ghetto or Jewish quarter of Venice. The failure of Venetian artillery against an invading French siege train at the end of the 15th century seems not to have resulted from inferior weapons but from French numerical strength and far greater mobility.

Venice on the Defensive

In 1509 Venice faced the League of Cambrai, which pitted most of Europe against her alone; among these foes was France, whose armies were among the most powerful of the day. Only two

River wall and bastion (left) of the 16th century defences of Kotor. The land walls may just be seen rising from left to right up the precipitous slopes of Mount Lovcen.

months after a huge explosion in the Arsenal's gunpowder store, Venice was defeated at the disastrous battle of Agnadello and the *Terra Firma* was lost. These territories were to be gradually and patiently regained; but the most remarkable aspect of this appalling year was, in fact, the Republic's survival.

From then on Venice adopted a grimly defensive stance, shunning all alliances and strengthening her frontiers with the most modern fortifications. The proportion of cavalry to infantry in her armies was drastically reduced, as in most other European states, while an ever-growing Ottoman naval threat to her overseas territories demanded ever more galleys, plus the marines and guns to fill them. On the other hand, Venetian military organisation became more and more conservative and predictable. Considerable efforts were devoted to avoiding war with the Ottomans and to maintaining strict neutrality in European affairs. The army and fleet co-operated more closely than ever. The former concentrated on mainland threats from Hapsburg Austria and Ottoman-ruled Bosnia, the latter on naval threats not only from the Ottomans but also from those champions of Christendom, the Spaniards, who now ruled southern Italy. Venice may have shrunk to a second-class power, but the wisdom of these policies resulted in the remarkably long life of her empire, which survived until Napoleon's takeover in 1797. Machiavelli's damning explanation of the Venetian defeat in 1509 as resulting from a 'miserable baseness of spirit caused

'The Story of St Ursula' by Carpaccio, 1493. *Left*—the pilgrims arrive at Cologne, showing fully armoured men equipped in Venetian style and an archer with a late Byzantine style of sword. *Below*—massacre of the pilgrims by Huns, showing lightly equipped soldiers who are probably based on Venetian *stradiotti*. (Academia Gall., Venice)

by a wretched military system' was proved wrong by survival for almost three more centuries against all the odds of European history.

One result of Venice's changed situation was a return to reliance, as far as possible, on her own men. Mercenaries were still recruited but such troops were now less available and Venice was also short of cash to pay them. The Venetian aristocracy remained small, never numbering more than 2,500 adult males, in comparison to its military, naval, political and administrative responsibilities. Ordinary people were now less willing to send their sons as soldiers, so that Venice was obliged to pardon criminals in return for their enlistment. The city increasingly relied on men from the *Terra Firma* which, despite its problems, was tied to Venice by a grudging sense of mutual advantage. The Venetians themselves remained a multi-cultural and even multi-racial society. Nevertheless there were still far more renegades from Christendom to Islam, and from Venice to the Ottomans, than vice-versa. Christians also treated their Muslim prisoner slaves far worse than Turks treated Christian slaves, largely because Christian society lacked the religious-legal sanctions to deal with such matters. Meanwhile the control of military affairs was concentrated in the hands of a college of experts much like a modern war council. Spies and informers played perhaps a greater rôle in Venetian military preparations than anywhere else in Europe, while in the 16th century Venice itself became a centre for the writing and printing of military books and maps. Military construction, skilled artisans, and above all the making of bronze cannon were increasingly concentrated in the Arsenal under the closest government supervision.

While the *Terra Firma* generally remained loyal to Venice, the eastern province of Friuli was still very backward and virtually feudal. It was here that Venice faced serious mainland threats from both Hapsburg Austria and the Turks. Both were, however, contained; and it would be fair to say that the Ottoman failure to conquer Italy, largely as a result of Venetian resistance, had a profound effect on the course of Renaissance and European history.

In 1615–17 Venice fought her last major land war, again against the Hapsburgs who, through Archduke Ferdinand of Austria, were protecting the troublesome Uskok pirates of Senj in the northern Adriatic.

Uskok and other pirates, plus a naval threat to Dalmatia from Spanish Naples, were the main problems confronting Venice in the late 16th and 17th centuries. The Uskoks claimed to be Crusaders fighting the Ottoman infidel, but in fact they caused more trouble to Christian Venice. Although their base at Senj was nominally in Hapsburg territory, the Uskoks were in reality freebooters. Nor were they the only pirates in the Adriatic: Spaniards, French, Dutch, English, Knights of Malta and Tuscan Knights of St Stephen all preyed on Venetian shipping. Muslim corsairs included Ottoman Turks, Muslims based in Albania and southern Dalmatia, as well as the famous Barbary Corsairs from North Africa. Yet they were not pirates in the true sense, since their activities, like those of Christian corsairs attacking Muslim shipping, were generally licensed by their respective governments.

Venetian woodcut showing the siege of Padua. Note the besiegers' use of cannon, handguns ignited by a second man with a heated *touche*, and the defenders' use of incendiary grenades (from Niccolò degli Agostini, *Li Successi Bellici* published in 1521).

'St George' by Carpaccio, *c.*1500. The saint is shown as a fully equipped Venetian man-at-arms, though without a helmet (*in situ* Scuola di S. Giorgio degle Schiavoni, Venice).

The main threat to Venice's overseas possessions naturally came from the Ottomans. The Empire *Da Mare* was thus divided into four defensive zones: the Gulf of Venice and Istria; Dalmatia and its islands; the Greek islands and Crete; and, far to the east, Cyprus, which had only fallen under Venetian control in 1489. Dalmatia served as the mainstay of Venetian naval power while the rest of the maritime empire retained its original strategic function as a chain of heavily defended bases, though the Ottomans had already broken through this chain in many places. There was also an increasing tendency for Venice's Greek and Balkan subjects to flee the ever heavier hand of Venetian colonial rule for the relative freedom of Ottoman territory. To some extent Venice was surviving on her past reputation. In fact, such was the awesome fame of the Arsenal that news of another devastating explosion in 1569 was said to have encouraged the Ottomans to invade, and ultimately seize Cyprus.

The Fleet

Defence of overseas bases still rested primarily on the galley fleet whose crews were still used as land or amphibious forces. *Sopracomiti* galley captains were the élite of the Venetian military establishment, with their wide experience not only of naval warfare but of gunnery and combat on land. Invariably of noble rank, their battle discipline was high but their sense of responsibility could at other times be poor. They frequently took their ships 'off station' on private voyages back to Venice; decorated their galley's poops with unauthorised and appallingly expensive gilded woodwork; constantly demanded new ships and generally treated their vessels as personal cruisers. In many ways these men, ferocious and skilful fighters as they were, had much in common both with medieval knights and with some air aces of the Great War!

Altogether, however, there was a steady decline in Venetian naval efficiency from the late 16th century onwards, despite a great victory over the Ottoman fleet at Lepanto in 1570. The shortage of crews became acute. Bigger warships, such as a 'great galley' flagship of 1601, carried 572 men, 290 being oarsmen, 132 being soldiers and their officers. Senior men fought in full armour, marines in lighter *corsaletti* of plate, while oarsmen wore light helmets and metal-lined *corrazzini* flexible body armour. Free oarsmen still helped the gunners in unskilled capacities, but Venice had already been obliged to lower her standards of naval recruitment in the mid-16th century. By the 17th century standards were sometimes abysmal. In 1539 conscription from the parishes had been abandoned in favour of quotas of oarsmen from the guilds and *Scuole* or religious fraternities. Albanians, Dalmatians, Greeks and Jews from Corfu included oarsmen who had simply been press-ganged. Convict oarsmen were brought, or even bought, from neighbouring states as far afield as Bavaria. Chained, ill-clothed, underfed and dying in large numbers from exposure, these convict oarsmen were nevertheless entrusted with weapons in battle. They remained much more important to the 17th century Venetian fleet than did true galley slaves. The latter could generally be distinguished by a Tartar-style single tuft of hair upon their heads, while the convicts were shaved bald.

Venice had for long put Christian prisoners to the oars while merely slaughtering all Muslim, renegade and Uskok prisoners, male or female. But the chronic shortage of oarsmen obliged Venice to follow other Christian navies by putting captured Turks on the benches. Huge numbers of Ottoman prisoners were, of course, available after the battle of Lepanto; and though the supply later dwindled, Christian fleets continued to use more galley-slaves than did the essentially volunteer-manned Muslim galleys. Mercy was still not shown to Ottoman officers, naval captains, skilled navigators or craftsmen, Venetian captains being instructed to ensure that such men were 'killed in whatever secret and discreet manner you see fit to use'.

The number of fighting men aboard a ship depended on where she was sailing. Though selected militia units were still used at sea, those who volunteered for such voyages were often desperate men, sea service being paid at lower rates than service on land. The impossibility of running away when fighting aboard ship meant that even inferior militiamen performed better at sea than on land. The *scapoli* were, strictly speaking, volunteer marines as distinct from the *soldati* who were troops raised in time of war for combat wherever needed, on land, sea or in amphibious campaigns. Such *soldati* were generally raised by *condottieri* mercenary leaders. Aristocratic volunteers were still recorded, but it is also clear that many such 'Nobles of the Quarterdeck' took their pay but never went to sea.

Early 17th century naval weapons included the longbow, which seems to have had a revival, whereas crossbows were generally abandoned in favour of handguns. Later steel-armed crossbows

'The Battle of Lepanto (1570)' painted by an anonymous artist shortly after the battle, one of the most detailed representations of the victory over the Ottomans. Note the galleys' heavy bow guns, the arquebus-men massed upon the decks, and the poorly clad galley-slaves. (Ham House, Victoria & Albert Mus., London)

The galley-harbour of Zadar (see plans of fortification), lying between the inner city (left) and the outer defences (right). Zadar was the main Venetian naval base in Dalmatia and this harbour could contain a small fleet of warships.

were remarkably accurate and immensely powerful, with a bow tension of over 3 kg, but they were slow and difficult to use, whereas anyone could blaze away with an arquebus or heavier musket at the short ranges of naval combat. Confusingly, however, naval handgunners were still often referred to as *balestieri* or crossbowmen.

Naval gunners formed the real élite. Graded in three ranks they were trained in the Scuola di Sta. Barbara in Venice, or in other artillery companies around the *Terra Firma* and overseas territories. They enjoyed numerous tax concessions, had the right to bear arms, and were responsible not only for the artillery but also for signal rockets and other incendiary devices. Fully trained gunners were, however, few (only 21 among a great galley's complement of 572) so other members of the crew had to help load, shift and even fire the guns. These

numbered from as little as 11 small guns on a light galley, up to 42 on a great galley, including a pair of culverins weighing over 10,000 lbs each. Most naval artillery seemed designed for ranges of 100 paces or more. The guns were placed in a galley's bows, being aimed by manoeuvring the ship itself. Breech-loaders were preferred for the lighter artillery since these could be loaded under cover without exposing their gunners to enemy short-range fire; and bronze cannon were valued, since they did not rust at sea. At its peak of efficiency the Venice Arsenal could fit out, arm and provision a newly built galley with standardised parts on a production-line basis unseen anywhere else until the Industrial Revolution.

Though fire-pots and other traditional incendiary devices were still being used, fundamental changes in naval gunnery were becoming apparent as efforts were made to sink or disable a foe with cannon alone. Light galleys had no part in this naval revolution, but they remained a vital element in the Venetian fleet. Their design was also steadily improved, with yet another system of rowing being introduced around 1534: known as *al scaloccio*, it reduced the number of now larger oars, each being pulled by a team of five to seven oarsmen. Various experimental warships were built in the late 16th century, but the most dramatic newcomer was the *galleas* which, developed from the old merchant great galley, had already put in an appearance at Lepanto. The *galleas* was a huge galley which served as a floating fortress in battle. Its cannon, often

The late 16th century Venetian fortress guarding Iraklion harbour, Crete. The low profile and thick walls were designed to resist artillery; above the entrance was a finely carved marble Lion of St Mark, the symbol of Venice.

1: Venetian knight, early 13th C.
2: Dalmatian urban militiaman, mid-13th C.
3: Dalmatian soldier, mid-13th C.

A

1: N. Italian crossbowman, c.1330
2: Italian armoured infantryman, c.1320
3: Knight, Collalto family, c.1340

B

1: Jacopo Cavalli, c.1380
2: Venetian infantryman, late 14th C.
3: Cavalli trumpeter, late 14th C.

C

1: Dalmatian crossbowman, c.1440
2: Dalmatian infantryman, c.1440
3: Dalmatian knight, mid-15th C.
4: Italian peasant levy, 15th C.

D

1: N. Italian crossbowman, late 15th C.
2: Venetian militiaman, late 15th C.
3: Venetian man-at-arms, late 15th C.

E

1: Stradiot, c.1500
2: Venetian light cavalryman, c.1500
3: Greek noble, early 16th C.

F

1: Venetian 'Bravo', late 16th C.
2: Escaped galley-slave, early 17th C.
3: Venetian knight, c.1600

G

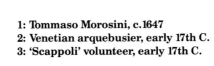

1: Tommaso Morosini, c.1647
2: Venetian arquebusier, early 17th C.
3: 'Scappoli' volunteer, early 17th C.

2   1   3

'Augustino Barbarigo', commander of the Venetian galleys at the battle of Lepanto, by the school of Titian, late 16th century. He wears the full uniform of a Venetian general. (Mus. Storico Navale, Venice)

mounted on wheeled carriages, were now ranged along its sides instead of being concentrated in the bow. Yet, despite occasional spectacular successes, the *galleas* was too slow and unwieldy to be widely useful and few were built.

The 16th century *galleon*, unlike its riverine namesake of an earlier century, was a slimmed-down version of the merchant 'round ship' and as such was an armed sailing vessel. It too could serve as a floating fortress in a major naval confrontation, but it was of little use against small pirate galleys in the confined spaces of the Dalmatian coast or Aegean islands. The superiority of northern pirate ships in the new warfare under sail led Venice to hire and eventually copy these vessels which were known to the Venetians as *bertoni*. Not until 1667 did Venice start building its own 'ships-of-the-line', using an English warship as a model, so far had sunk the one-time 'Mistress of the Seas'.

With the consolidation of Ottoman power throughout the Balkans and Middle East, and Venice's policy of avoiding alliances, the Venetian empire was more isolated than ever. Strategy, as well as the cost of updating fortifications, was increasingly concentrated on the major anchorages: Zadar, Sibenik, Kotor, Corfu, Iraklion, Kyrenia, Famagusta and Nicosia. Corfu, described as 'the heart and soul of this state', was the lynch-pin of the entire empire. From here anti-piracy patrols as well as great fleets could operate. True blockades were still impossible with available naval technology while, in turn, vessels as powerful as the *galleas* could almost always force their way through Ottoman resistance with supplies for distant Venetian outposts. Modern artillery also enabled bigger merchant ships to defend themselves, so it was the smaller ships that suffered most from pirates and corsairs.

Land Warfare

On land major tactical changes had altered the face of European warfare in the early 16th century, with great armies now seeking a decisive blow rather than indulging in the elaborate manoeuvre and attrition of previous centuries. Far higher casualties were suffered than had been normal in medieval and early Renaissance warfare. Yet this was a passing phase, because improvements in fortification techniques soon bogged down tactics once again. Meanwhile the Venetians clung to their traditionally cautious approach, making great use of their mountainous northern frontiers against both Austrians and Ottomans. Tactics varied, though Venetian armies sometimes marched with light cavalry in the van followed by heavy cavalry and infantry. Artillery formed a central body while a second corps of infantry, heavy and light cavalry brought up the rear, their order being the reverse of those in the van. *Stradioti* were naturally employed as advance and flanks guards. Many *condottieri* leaders still offered considerable loyalty to Venice, while the supposedly civilian *proveditori* took an increasingly important rôle in positions of command. At their head a *Proveditor General* had his own guard of 12 to 25 halberdiers, plus a full staff. Other *proveditori* commanded the light cavalry and *stradioti*, while a special corps of *Proveditori alle Fortezze* was established in 1542 to supervise the Republic's fixed defences. Others armed and trained the peasant volunteers of the Treviso area, controlled the licensed pillaging of enemy territory, the allocation of artillery or the surveying of frontiers. The Arsenal was also run by *proveditori*, though it proved far easier to manufacture enough weapons than to get them to the troops where and when they were needed.

The army itself still included militias from Venice and the *Terra Firma*, and many members of the poorer aristocracy had little choice but to become soldiers. Yet the overall quality of Venetian armies had declined badly by the early 17th century. Heavy cavalry in full plate armour and riding 'barded' or armoured horses were anachronistic in this new age of firearms but they were retained, though in decreasing numbers, for reasons of prestige and to give the richer aristocracy a sense of military purpose. Such heavy cavalry were still organised in *lanzi* of one man-at-arms, two lightly armed riders with spear or crossbow, and a mounted servant. Efforts to recruit noblemen as light cavalry were only partially successful, though the issuing of heavy men-at-arms with a pair of pistols did prolong their military rôle. By the 17th century, cavalry lance and sword had finally been abandoned in favour of pistol and sword. The gun, normally now a reliable wheellock weapon that needed no match, would be fired just before contact with the foe, whereupon the sword would be drawn. Such tactics were, however, costly in horses.

During the early part of the 16th century, Venetian light cavalry of Italian origin were mostly armed with crossbows or arquebuses and, unlike the *stradioti*, fought more as mounted infantry than real cavalry. Many of those involved in the almost guerrilla warfare of the Friulian frontier carried small matchlock handguns, ancestors of the true pistol. Others, called *cavalleria leggiera*, wore plated half-armour, were organised in *lanzi* similar to those of the heavy cavalry, and similarly fought with spears, maces and swords. True light cavalry or *cappeletti* were mostly of Croatian or Balkan origin, though they remained distinct from the more famous *stradioti*. By the late 16th century many *stradioti* were being armed with wheellock carbines and a small amount of body armour, arquebus-proofed on the front, pistol-proofed on the back and with a pistol-proof helmet.

Relatively rich and peaceful, Venice now lacked foot soldiers rather than cavalry. The *Scuole* and guilds did supply some infantry units but were more important as sources of oarsmen, while the *Arsenalotti* still offered volunteers in addition to the

Doge's Palace Guard. The *Terra Firma* cities selected gate guards from their own citizens as well as militias to supplement professional garrison troops. In peacetime these garrisons were themselves responsible for guarding gates, piazzas, food and ammunition stores, patrolling the walls, streets and sloping glacis beyond the wall, and manning the citadel. Some cities like Brescia also raised an indigenous force of *guardaroli* to take over some patrol duties.

Militias were, however, of very varied quality. Most consisted of men enlisted between the ages of 17 and 24 who remained liable for service for eight years. They were organised in sub-companies of around 100 men who trained five Sundays a year. These in turn formed part of a larger company of up

A

to 600 militiamen which held annual manoeuvres. People joined for a variety of reasons, though permission to bear arms and exemption from labour service on the fortifications or in clearing canals were common motives. In some of the wilder or mountainous regions like Friuli people habitually carried arms in any case, and they could be enlisted when necessary as rural guerrillas armed with bow and arrow.

The crossbow declined in favour as an infantry weapon, as it had done at sea; while the barely trained militias were rarely competent to fight with pikes, which was a technique demanding firm discipline and much practice. Primitive *schioppeti* handguns were still employed in the 16th century though the arquebus gradually superceded them. Heavier muskets, requiring forks to support them, soon made an appearance among the militia. Men were trained to fire arquebuses both running and crouching, at targets 40 paces distant; musketeers trained with targets at twice that range. Other training involved all the usual advancing, retiring and skirmishing techniques of late 16th and 17th century infantry warfare. Coloured surcoats and

sashes, agreed war-cries and known banners all helped maintain cohesion in battle, while a few militia units even wore the red and white uniform livery of the Venetian Captain General.

Venice's militias may have been more effective than those of other European nations, yet their real value appears to have been moral rather than military. They fostered a sense of national identity and proved that the Republic trusted its own people in arms, a rare feature in the 16th and 17th centuries.

Mid-16th century Venetian cavalry sometimes carried arquebus soldiers into battle riding pillion. By the early 17th century arquebusiers, also carrying pistols, were operating as true mounted infantry; a small élite of mounted infantry armed with wheellock muskets were recorded in 1616. Troops of such volunteer 'dragoons' were similarly raised by noble *signori*, until the government realised that these men were often no more than mounted *bravi* or thugs in the pay of aristocratic families. Private armies of *bravi* were now a problem throughout Italy and seem to have become a real threat to public order in Venice. Many were

Woodcuts of Venetian military costumes in Cesare Vecellio's *Habiti antichi et modernii di tutti il Mondo* **published in 1598. A—heavy cavalry man-at-arms; B—light cavalryman (lance only partly shown); C—soldier from the Sfakia region of southern Crete; D—*Galeotti* or *Falila* conscript soldier aboard war-galley.**

B   C   D

'Unknown Venetian nobleman' by Moroni, mid-16th century, showing the arming jacket with mail panels to protect the armpits. This was worn beneath plate-armour, here lying around the man's feet. (Nat. Gall., London)

who were even credited with murdering their enemies with poison-filled glass *stilettos*.

While troops from Venice and the *Terra Firma* served in the overseas empire and suffered terrible losses from disease and exposure, troops from the empire also fought for Venice in Italy. The *stradioti* above all achieved some notable successes against French heavy cavalry in 1516. In fact Venice made great efforts to enlarge the overseas army *Da Mare* and to improve the quality of colonial militias. The standard of these militia forces remained low, however, and their equipment was often abysmal. In Corfu, Crete and Cyprus local troops were trained to use the arquebus, but many continued to fight with composite bows in Turkish fashion. Militias in smaller islands like Kefallinia sometimes signed up merely to avoid starvation. Elsewhere, as on the Catholic and fiercely pro-Venetian island of Tinos, strange relics of a medieval feudal system of recruitment survived. A poorly paid local castle-guard of *paghe da guazzo* sometimes included Venetian troops who had settled overseas on a tiny pension and with minimal duties. Above all, however, there remained the famed *stradioti*. Fierce and outlandishly dressed, brittle on points of honour and addicted to plunder, they still fought primarily with light spears, swords and composite bows. They tended to shy away from European or Ottoman infantry with firearms, but proved highly effective against Turkish cavalry who fought in much the same style as themselves. By the late 16th and early 17th centuries, however, many *stradioti* were themselves adopting pistols and cavalry carbines.

Inevitable variations in the military styles of the differing Venetian possessions also persisted. The *stradioti* of Dalmatia were based in eight main centres, though they spent most of their time in out-stations closer to the frontier. One hundred *stradioti* were based at Corfu with detachments on other Ionian islands, while the *stradioti* of Crete were of poor quality, partly because of a scarcity of horses in the eastern Mediterranean. The fearsome *Sfakioti* infantry archers from southern Crete sometimes fought for Venice, but were generally a source of rebels, brigands and pirates. With a growing threat of Ottoman attack, the Venetian authorities tried to reform the chaotic and corrupt Cretan militia system and to erect modern fortifications. Anti-

themselves drawn from desperate and impoverished noble families; others had been mercenary soldiers and numbered foreigners among their ranks. A ban on the carrying of weapons within Venice had little effect. Large-scale brawls were frequent and even involved the use of arquebuses, while duels and assassinations with the slender *stiletto* dagger became a *bravi* speciality. Things got so bad that some people took to wearing light mail protection beneath their clothes. An undeserved and romantic mythology developed around these Venetian *bravi*,

Venetian feeling was, however, rife throughout the island and when the Ottoman assault did come many Cretans welcomed the invader.

Venetian rule appears to have been even harsher in Cyprus than Crete. For Venice, Cyprus never became anything more than a dangerous military outpost where Venetians were not only unpopular but were notably reluctant to serve. Cyprus already had a very mixed population. The Venetian authorities came to a reasonable understanding with the existing Catholic military élite which dated from the late 12th century Crusader conquest of the island, and which already included many Italians. The Venetians also favoured the basically Arab Maronite Christian community whose roots went even deeper; but they seem to have failed to win many friends among the large and warlike Armenian minority. It is also interesting to note that many of both these minorities later converted to Islam following the Ottoman conquest of the island in 1571, becoming the ancestors of at least part of the present day Turkish-Cypriot community. Mainland Greek *stradioti* were brought into Venetian Cyprus, and by 1519 a number of Cypriot Greeks had also been enlisted. These men served alongside the *turcopoli* light cavalry retainers of the old landed aristocracy, troops whose history similarly went back at least as far as the Crusades.

In addition to volunteers and militias from Venice, the *Terra Firma* and the overseas possessions, 16th and 17th century Venetian armies contained a large number of mercenaries. Most *condottieri* troops, in other words those recruited as an entire contract unit, came from the *Terra Firma* or elsewhere in northern Italy. Other regional soldiers included Corsicans and Ligurians, while non-Italians numbered Swiss, Germans, (most Venetian gunners outside the navy still being German) French, Spaniards, Czechs, Dutch, Flemish and English among their ranks. The majority served as infantry whereas most, though not all, Balkan mercenaries were cavalry. The latter were recruited not only from Venetian territory but also from neighbouring Ottoman-ruled regions. Apart from the Catholic Croatians most were Orthodox Christians, but some were of unspecified religious affiliation and a few were clearly Muslims from Bosnia and Albania. This scandalised Venice's neighbours while even the Venetian diarist

Detail from 'Gypsy and Soldier' by Caravaggio, late 16th century, showing a typical Italian sword of the period. (Louvre, Paris)

Girolamo Priuli noted that, for Venice, such recruitment was like a man 'cutting off his penis to spite his wife'. The discrimination that these 'Turks' faced in camp soon led them to abandon Venetian service, however.

Siege and counter-siege

Venetian use of parallel trench systems when besieging an enemy stronghold may themselves show Ottoman influence (see MAA 140, *Armies of the Ottoman Turks 1300–1774*), and the Venetians were clearly willing to learn from any source. Captured guns were tested and the Arsenal constantly experimented with new designs. There was a gradual move towards smaller and more mobile artillery while field guns and siege trains were now clearly separate. The most dramatic developments were, however, in fortification. This was a field in which 16th century Italy influenced the rest of Europe.

Venice had adopted a defensive neutral stance in which fortifications played a vital rôle. The northern and eastern mountain passes could be blocked to an enemy siege train with strategically sited fortresses, even if infantry could always infiltrate around such defences, but the broad Lombard plain had always been extremely difficult to defend. Venetian strategists now took into consideration the rivers that sliced their territory into sections, while the towers of strategic cities were lowered and their gates strengthened to take account of powerful new siege artillery. Castellans were responsible for the munitions, artillery and garrisons of such towns, but the poor pay meant that few of the military élite accepted such posts.

The 14th–15th century defences of Ston, said to be the longest city walls in Europe. This was one of the most strongly fortified positions in Dalmatia and was frequently disputed between Venice and Dubrovnik. The 'long walls' enclose the mountain-top, the port of Mali Ston on the far side of the hill, and the main settlement of Veliki Ston (here). Low round artillery bastions (lower left) were added at a later date.

It was the defences themselves that, by the mid-16th century, eventually solidified Venice's frontiers. One new concept that the Venetians used early in the 16th century was the 'double Pisan rampart' in which a besieger, if he broke through the outer wall, found himself facing a second rampart and trapped in a fire-swept killing zone. Basically, however, the new system of defences relied on wider and deeper stone-lined ditches, and flanking fire from projecting bastions which, being low, broad and earth-filled, could not easily be destroyed by artillery or even mines. Paradoxically, the development of really effective gunpowder artillery had strengthened the defensive element in warfare rather than the offensive. The medieval castle had become a Renaissance fortress but it still held the upper hand, while hand-guns fired by masses of barely trained defenders could have a devastating effect on any attackers who managed to force a breach. However, these modern defences needed wide open fire zones, which led to the ruthless demolition of built-up areas both inside and outside their walls. The long-established re-

lationship between an Italian city and its surrounding *contado* also changed. The countryside was now generally abandoned to an enemy raider while defence was concentrated in the city which was in turn swollen by refugees from the villages. Fear of sedition and insurrection within the walls then led to a strengthening of the citadel as a defence within a defence.

The earliest such fortifications were built in a hurry and of earth, so that little now remains. It is the stone defences that replaced them which now give a special character to many north Italian towns. The vital city of Verona, for example, was refortified in the 1530s, being given an immensely strong citadel on the hills above. Thereafter Verona never endured another serious attack until 1797, though as early as 1598 the authorities faced the encroachment on the artillery fire zones of sheds, houses, orchards, vegetable plots, drainage ditches and bird-snaring groves (the Veronese still like their *uccelletti*—grilled small birds—served on a bed of maize flour). Among those military engineers who designed Verona's new defences was Michele di

Courtyard of the Porta di Udine (1605), the best preserved of Palmanova's three gates (see plans of fortifications). This fortress, designed by Savorgnano and Scamozzi in 1593 and built on a virgin site to protect Venetian territory from Austrian or Ottoman attack, is the most perfectly preserved example of late Renaissance military architecture in existence.

Fortifications in the *Terra Firma* (Mainland Territories): *A—*Verona *c.*1600 showing improvements designed by Michele Sanmichele *c.*1530 (note that the Baluardo di Campo Marzo was added at the end of the 16th C.); *B—*Orzinuovi mid-16th C. (after plan *c.*1600); *C—*reconstruction of the Venetian Arsenal in the early 14th C. showing the first *Corderie* rope-factory (after Pizzarello & Fontana); *D—*Palmanova, designed by Giulio Savorgnano & Vincenzo Scamozzi in 1593 (after plan *c.*1600); *E—*Malano, double-octagon bastion on an artificial island in the Venice Lagoon near Malamocco (after plan *c.*1600); *F—*Baluardo di S. Bernardino, one of Verona' bastions rebuilt to Sanmichele's design around 1530 (after Duffy).

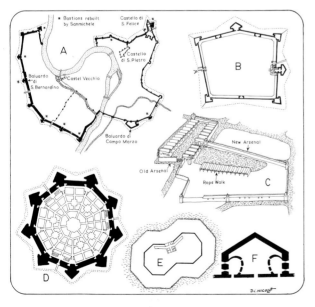

Sanmicheli. He had studied the work of another master, Antonio da Sangallo, and was to have his own famous followers; such engineering 'dynasties' became a feature of Venetian and Italian military architecture in the 16th and 17th centuries. A classic fortification of this period, at Palmanova, still stands virtually unchanged not far from the Yugoslav border. It was planned in 1593 as a supposedly self-sufficient military town within a symmetrical nine-bastioned wall, built in virgin territory as the hub of Friulian defence against Austrians and Ottomans. Palmanova was completed in the early 1600s, but remained such a lonely and unhealthy site that for years no one wanted to live there.

The 17th century saw another burst of fortification-building around Venice and overseas. The fortifications of the empire *Da Mare* had, in fact, been overlooked for years, but though they were small and old fashioned they had generally been well maintained. Such defences faced attack from both land and sea, and it was fortunate that the Ottomans had been relatively quiet for some time. One major problem was that the cost of new construction had to be borne largely by the local communities and these were tiny, except in Crete and Cyprus. In Dalmatia the Ottomans had already broken through to the sea in a number of places, while the Uskoks and Hapsburgs made uncomfortable neighbours. Venetian fortifications such as Kotor also had to keep an eye on the wild Montenegrans who, though fiercely anti-Ottoman, also craved a sea outlet of their own. Only the main naval bases were given new and modern fortifications; but when the crisis came in the 1640s Venice did unexpectedly well. Dalmatia was easy to reinforce from nearby Venice and was studded with castles, whereas the Ottomans were operating far from their main bases, across bleak mountains inhabited by *Morlacchi* peasants who were all too eager to revolt against their nominal Turkish overlords. The Ottoman attacks were, in fact, defeated and Venice managed to expand her territory.

In Cyprus the Venetians made great efforts to strengthen their position shortly before the Ottomans attacked. At first their plans betrayed a typical Renaissance preoccupation with elaborate machinery, seeming to put their faith in ropes, pulleys and counter-weights, hidden explosive mines and multi-barrelled fire projectors designed to rear up in an attacker's face, not to mention slow-release poisons in neighbouring wells and baited fodder for enemy horses. In the event preference was given to strengthening the fortifications of Nicosia; this entailed the virtual destruction of the old city, including the royal tombs and monastery of San Domenico, and the building of a seven-bastioned five-mile-circuit wall similar to that recently erected at Iraklion in Crete. Yet in 1571 Nicosia fell to the Ottomans after a siege of less than five months.

Venetian defences proved more effective in Crete where Iraklion endured a 22-year Ottoman siege. The Turkish invasion was actually sparked by the piratical aggression of the Knights of St John based on Malta, though it was Venice that paid the price. The war was long and bitter, ranging from Dalmatia to the Dardanelles. The Ottomans eventually took Crete, though the Venetians fought with a fanaticism excelling even that of the Turks; the commander of the fortress of St Theodore was said to have blown up himself, his men, and the attackers when the Ottomans finally overran his defences.

The Ottomans had already unsuccessfully attempted to take Corfu in 1537. Between 1549 and 1570 the Venetian government paid no less than 250,000 ducats to strengthen that island's fortifications, which easily repulsed a final Ottoman assault in 1716. Only one year earlier the last Venetian-held Aegean island, the lonely outpost of Tinos, had finally fallen. The Venetian empire was once again reduced to those possessions west of Greece that had been held since before the Fourth Crusade, plus Corfu and the Ionian islands which, early in the 19th century, passed to another rising imperial and naval power—Britain.

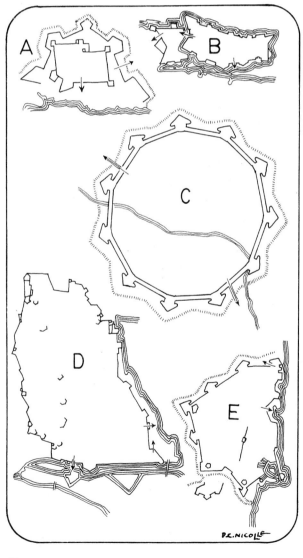

Fortifications in the *Imperio da Mar* (Overseas Territories): A—Split, Dalmatia (after carved plan on façade of S. Maria del Giglio, Venice); B—Zadar, Dalmatia (after carved plan on façade of S. Maria del Giglio, Venice); C—Nicosia, Cyprus (after late 16th C. plan); D—Kotor, Dalmatia (after late 17th C. plan); E—Iraklion, Crete (after carved plan on façade of S. Maria del Giglio, Venice, & 17th C. plans).

One of the surviving bastions of Nicosia. In 1567 Venice greatly reduced the size of this city, and though the Venetian fortifications survive they appear to have been extensively modernised during the Ottoman period. (Courtesy of Cypriot Press & Information Office)

Arms and Armour

Venice never became one of the major arms-producing centres of Europe, but its commercial wealth and wide trade contacts ensured that Venetian troops were usually well equipped. Weapons as well as ships were, of course, made in the Arsenal, and the government also standardised the design of vital items like crossbows so that crossbow strings and bolts or arrows would fit all weapons. These had composite arms similar in structure to the powerful composite bows of the Muslim world. They were also exported to the Balkans via Venetian Dalmatia at least as early as the 14th century. By this time the demand for things like crossbow bolts was so high that in 1304 the Venetian government had to sub-contract the manufacture of 20,000 iron bolt-heads needed by Venetian communal forces. Experimentation with new weapons reflected a scientific attitude perhaps inherited from the Byzantines. A multi-shot crossbow, supposedly capable of shooting 15 bolts and comparable to one also seen in a late 12th century Islamic military treatise, was recorded in the 13th century. Such an impractical multi-shot crossbow was again suggested in 1411, by which

time the Venetian Arsenal was also experimenting with ways of improving the new handguns.

Venice similarly exported swords, helmets and other pieces of armour to the Balkans and perhaps beyond. Venice herself was open to influences from the East, the European coat-of-plates possibly being inspired by Byzantine or Islamic lamellar armour brought to Europe via Venice and its colonial empire. Nor were influences all from the East. The broad *basilard* dagger which became a major weapon of Venetian infantry was, in contrast, probably of Swiss or south German origin, its name indicating that the first such daggers were imported from Basel. The popularity of both hardened and 'soft' or flexible leather armour in Venice and the rest of Italy could also betray Byzantine or Islamic influence.

Milan rather than Venice had, however, been the main centre of arms production in northern Italy since the mid-13th century. Milan made armours designed specifically for export, including the so-called Venetian style of sallet and barbuta helmets. Yet there were other important arms-manufacturing centres in northern Italy, and from the mid-14th century, some of these lay within the expanding Venetian *Terra Firma*. For centuries the Italian arms industry was the most important in Europe, though partially completed weapons were imported from other sources to be assembled in northern Italy. It might also be mentioned that the arms industry employed women as well as men, women being recorded as 'sewing' helmets and armour. This probably referred to the linings or decoration of helmets and to the numerous leather straps of later medieval armour. By the mid-15th century Milan itself was in decline and Venice controlled all the remaining north Italian arms centres. German armourers gradually seized domination of the European market from the mid-16th century, but these Venetian manufacturing centres continued to make huge quantities of fine armours, weapons and above all firearms. They certainly retained a special place in the market for elaborately decorated ceremonial arms.

The chief such Venetian armaments centre was Brescia, which took over from Milan as the main Italian producer late in the 16th and 17th centuries. Brescia had, in fact, been manufacturing arms since the 11th and possibly even 8th century. Venice took

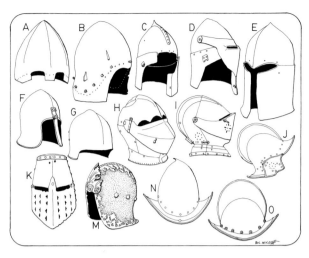

Helmets: *A*—Mid-14th C. Venetian bascinet, cut down & with eye-slots added in 15th C., found at Khalkis (Met. Mus. of Art, New York); *B*—typical north Italian barbuta, *c.*1350 (Mus. Poldi Pezzoli, Milan); (*C–G* Venetian helmets found at Khalkis, now in Historical Mus., Athens) *C*—helmet with hinged right cheek-piece missing, *c.*1500–50; *D*—visored helmet with hinged right cheek-piece missing, *c.*1500–50; *E*—so-called 'Corinthian' salet, mid-15th C.; *F*—salet with hinged nasal, mid-15th C.; *G*—small salet, mid-15th C.; *H*—Milanese armet, late 15th C., (Mus. Civ. Marzoli, Brescia); *I*—Milanese close helmet, decoration not shown, *c.*1570 (Mus. Civ. Marzoli, Brescia); *J*—burgonet, decoration not shown, late 16th C. (Mus. Civ. Marzoli); *K*—Great Helm from Bolzano, *c.*1300 (Castel S. Angelo Mus., Rome); *M*—*barbuta alla veneziana* covered in red velvet & with gilded bronze ornamentation, late 15th C. (Mus. Civ. Marzoli, Brescia); *N–O*—pointed & crested morions, decoration not shown, late 16th C. (Armoury of Doge's Palace, Venice)

the city in 1426 and thereafter encouraged the Brescian industry, drawing in armourers from Milan who hoped to escape the heavy hand of Visconti rule. Not until 1644 was the Brescian guild of armourers dissolved, and even that did not mark the end of fine Brescian arms production. Apart from incredibly richly decorated 17th century armours, Brescian guns earned a fine reputation; this was particularly true of Brescian wheellock pistols and muskets. Such 'self-firing' guns, which were much more reliable than the previous matchlocks, appear to have been invented in Germany. For years they were considered so threatening to law and order that they were declared illegal, not being permitted even for military use until 1570. Nevertheless wheellocks had reached Venice via her eastern *Terra Firma* province of Friuli early in the 1530s, and thereafter the complicated new firing mechanisms were imported from Germany to be made up into guns at Brescia. The finished weapons were then re-exported all over Europe and the Balkans.

Further Reading

General histories of Venice are easily available. Listed below are some more specialised sources.

Arms & Armour:

U. Franzoi, *Armoury of the Doge's Palace* (Venice n.d.)

A. Gaibi, 'L'Arte bresciane delle armature: contributo alla storia della armi defensive italiane', *Armi Antiche* (1963), pp.15–50.

F. Rossi, *Armi e armaioli bresciani del '400* (Brescia 1971).

Heraldry:

E. Del Torso, *Araldica Civica del Friuli* (Udine 1978)

E. Morando, *Libro d'Arme di Venezia* (Verona 1979).

E. Morando, *Armoriale Veronese* (Verona 1976).

Fortification:

A. Della Valle (edit.), *Venezia e i Turchi, Scontri e confronti di due civiltà* (Milan 1985), includes articles on fortification & military confrontation.

G. Gerola, *I monumenti venete nell'isola di Creta*, 5 vols (Venice 1906–32)

P. Marchesi, *Fortezze Veneziane 1508–1797* (Milan 1984).

U. Pizzarello & V. Fontana, *Pietre e Legni dell'Arsenale di Venezia* (Venice 1983).

Military organisation:

J. R. Hale, 'Men and Weapons: The Fighting Potential of Sixteenth-Century Venetian Galleys,' in *War and Society: A Yearbook of Military History* edit. B. Bond & I. Roy (London 1975), pp.1–23.

M. B. Mallett & J. R. Hale, *The Military Organization of a Renaissance State: Venice c.1400 to 1617* (Cambridge 1984).

A. Tenenti, *Piracy & the Decline of Venice* (London 1961).

The Plates

A: The 13th century

A1: Venetian knight, early 13th century

During the early 13th century Venetian arms and armour were basically the same as those of the rest of Italy. Earlier Byzantine influence had largely disappeared and there had as yet been little oriental influence from the Venetian overseas empire. On the other hand Italian styles themselves differed from those of northern Europe. This knight wears a full mail hauberk, though lacks the surcoat which had become normal in France. His legs are protected by standard mail chausses but beneath his mail coif is a close-fitting iron *cervellière* helmet with a very large nasal to protect his face. The knight's large shield would also have been unusual outside Italy and might reflect the importance that archery had already achieved in Italian warfare. (Main sources: carved frieze, late 12th–early 13th C., facade of Fidenza Cathedral; wall paintings, late 12th C., Palazzo della Ragione, Mantua; carved ivory throne, 1212–50, Mus. Nazionale, Ravenna.)

A2: Dalmatian urban militiaman, mid-13th century
The military styles of Dalmatia were a strange mixture of Balkan and Italian fashions. The large flat-bottomed shield used by his unarmoured infantryman would have been considered old-fashioned in Western Europe; but the buttons on his tunic were a very modern idea that had hardly yet appeared in the West. His soft, flat-topped hat seems to suggest a Hungarian style from the neighbouring Hungarian-ruled interior. (Main source: carved reliefs, c.1240, west door of Trogir Cathedral.)

A3: Dalmatian soldier, mid-13th century
This man's equipment is similar to that worn in medieval Serbia and even parts of Byzantium. It consists of a brimmed iron *chapel-de-fer* over a broad mail coif that also protected the man's shoulders. In addition to a mail hauberk he has an iron lamellar cuirass of clearly Eastern or Byzantine inspiration. His sword is, however, typically European. (Main source: *Guards at the Holy Sepulchre*, carved relief, c.1240, west door of Trogir Cathedral.)

B: The first half of the 14th century
B1: North Italian crossbowman, c.1330
Crossbowmen played an essential rôle in 14th century Italian warfare and many appear to have been professional mercenaries. Even urban militia crossbowmen would generally have been well-equipped by their rich cities. This man is a typical example, with his strong iron sallet helmet with a hinged nasal; thickly padded mail tippet over neck and shoulder, and mail hauberk over a thickly quilted gambeson. He is armed not only with a manually-loaded crossbow but with a broad basilard dagger. (Main sources: carved capitals, early 14th C., Doge's Palace, Venice; *Crucifixion cycle* wall paintings, c.1330–50, church of Sant' Abbondio, Como.)

B2: Italian armoured infantryman, c.1320
This man is obviously a professional, either a titled knight or a successful mercenary. He carries a broad-brimmed one piece iron *chapel-de-fer* and has an early form of coat-of-plates over his mail. The leg-protecting greaves are of hardened leather, and his sabatons (armoured shoes) also appear to be covered in hardened leather. His sword, the slender basilard dagger at his belt and long-bladed guisarme axe are common weapons; but the barbed javelins standing ready for use would usually only be for war at sea. (Main source: *St Martin renounces the sword* by Simone Martini, c.1317, Montefiore Chapel, church of St Francis, Assisi.)

'Parade of the General di Mare in Piazza San Marco', early 17th century engraving by Giacomo Franco. (Mus. Civ. Correr, Venice)

B3: Venetian knight of the Collalto family, c.1340
Here a young member of the warlike Collalto family from Venice's *Terra Firma* mainland possessions, is not only armoured in the latest Italian style but also wears a headcloth that does not appear to have been worn outside Italy. His bascinet helmet has its mail aventail doubled over in another Italian fashion; while his fabric-covered coat-of-plates and shoulder flaps would probably have been lined with iron or cuir-bouilli—hardened leather scales. The rerebraces that protect his upper arms would probably have metal elements inside, as would the cuffs of his buff leather gauntlets. The greaves that protect only the front of his legs are now of iron. (Main sources: carved capitals, early 14th C., Doge's Palace, Venice; effigy of Bernardino dei Baranzoni, *c.*1345–50 Mus. Lapidario Estense, Modena; supporting figures on tomb of Azzone Visconti, *c.*1339 church of S. Gottardo in Corte, Milan.)

C: The second half of the 14th century
C1: Jacopo Cavalli, c.1380
Jacopo Cavalli here wears a heavy, crested great helm that would normally have been reserved for parades. Only the shoulder defences of his coat-of-plates are now visible, the rest being obscured beneath a tight-fitting surcoat. The knight's iron arm-protecting rerebraces, couters and vambraces only cover the outside of the limbs, and the iron poleyns and greaves on his legs are of a similarly light type. His shield now has a notched lance-rest in one corner. His horse is protected by a small amount of armour, consisting of an iron chamfron with extra neck lames, a quilted crinet on the neck and a small crupper over the animal's rump. (Main sources: tomb of Federico Cavalli, late 14th C., church of S. Anastasia, Verona; tomb of Cansignoro della Scala, *c.*1350–75 outside church of S. Maria Antiqua, Verona; Battle of Val di Chiana, wall painting 1373, Palazzo Publico, Siena.)

C2: Venetian infantryman, late 14th century
Only the upper arm rerebraces are now made of hardened leather, the leg harness being all of iron, as are the splints inside his lower arm vambraces and his fabric-covered solid breatplate. The deep fluted bascinet is a typically Italian helmet, but appears to be worn over an old-fashioned mail coif. The large rectangular red mantlet bearing the golden Lion of St Mark was, of course, solely an infantry shield. The broad-bladed spear is a Balkan weapon, perhaps imported from Dalmatia. (Main sources: tomb of Manno Donati, late 14th C., church of S. Antonio, Padua; *Naval battle between Venetian and Imperial forces*, wall painting by Spinello Aretino mid-14th C., Palazzo Publico, Siena; *Story of St James*, reliefs on silver altar by Leonardo di Ser Giovanni 1371, Pistoia Cathedral.)

C3: Trumpeter in service of the Cavalli family, late 14th century
This trumpeter wears no armour save for a light mail hauberk, and a deep helmet which has a hinged cheek-piece, perhaps originally intended for an archer. The man's dagger again perhaps shows Balkan influence. (Main sources: Venetian helmet from Khalkis, late 14th–early 15th C., Historical

'Francesco Morosini' wearing the Doge's cap and a senior commander's cloak with shoulder decorations, by Giovanni Carboncino mid-17th century. (Mus. Civ. Correr, Venice)

QVATER CONTRA TVRCAS IMPERATOR
BIS IMPERATOR SIMVL ET REIPVBLICÆ PRINCEPS

Mus., Athens; *Battle of Val di Chiana*, wall painting 1373, Palazzo Publico, Siena.)

D: Crossing the Lóppio Pass, 1439
D1: Dalmatian crossbowman, c.1440

By the 15th century various systems of spanning more powerful crossbows had come into use: here a cranequin is shown. This Dalmatian soldier has another deep helmet with a hinged cheek-piece on the right side. He otherwise wears full plate armour on his arms, legs and body, though the latter is covered by a quilted surcoat in somewhat Burgundian style. (Main sources: relief carving mid-15th C., Jurja Barakovica street, Sibenik; Venetian helmet from Khalkis, first half 15th C., Historical Mus., Athens.)

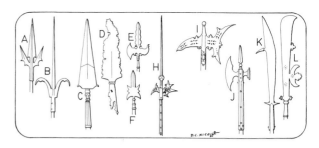

Staff weapons: *A—ronco*, 16th–17th C. (Armoury of Doge's Palace, Venice); *B—ronco*, 16th C. (Mus. Civ. Marzoli, Brescia); *C*—ceremonial partizan, decoration not shown, early 17th C. (Mus. Civ. Marzoli, Brescia); *D*—remains of broad-bladed spear or partizan found in ford near Trilj, Dalmatia, undated (Archaeological Mus., Split); *E–F*—halberd-partizans for officers, 17th C. (Armoury of Doge's Palace, Venice); *H*—ceremonial halberd, late 16th C. (Mus. Civ. Marzoli, Brescia); *I*—ceremonial halberd, 16th C. (Armoury of Doge's Palace, Venice); *J*—pole-axe, 16th C. (Armoury of Doge's Palace, Venice); *K*—glaive, 15th–16th C. (Mus. Civ. Marzoli, Brescia); *L*—ceremonial glaive, decoration not shown, Venetian 17th C. (Mus. Civ. Marzoli, Brescia).

D2: Dalmatian infantryman, c.1440

Here a helmet with a hinged cheek-piece also has a moveable visor. This time the surcoat is of rich brocade imported from the Islamic world. The strap supporting the rondel dagger goes to a belt worn beneath the surcoat. The man's armour is again of full iron plate with a minimum of mail; and the large triangular shield is an infantry form that had been used in the Balkans for some centuries. (Main sources: relief carving mid-15th C., Jurja Barakovica street, Sibenik; Venetian helmet from Khalkis, first half of 15th C., Historical Mus., Athens.)

D3: Venetian colonial knight from Sibenik, Dalmatia, mid-15th century

Though he is a Dalmatian and wears a form of headdress betraying Hungarian influence, this knight has the best imported Italian armour. Typical would be a sallet helmet in a specifically Venetian style, covered in velvet and with golden decorations riveted to the surface. Note the extra fringe of mail from the rim of the fauld fastened to the lower edge of his breastplate. (Main sources: statue of knight early 15th C., Orlandov Kip, Dubrovnik; *Missal* of Duke Hrvoje Vukcic Hrvatinic of Split, Topkapi Lib., Istanbul.)

D4: Italian peasant levy, 15th century

Longbows of simple construction were regarded as peasant weapons in late medieval Italy. On the other hand some of the best yew wood for such bows was grown in Italy, being exported in large quantities to England. (Main source: bronze door by Ghiberti mid-15th C., Baptistery, Florence.)

E: The second half of the 15th century
E1: Northern Italian crossbowman, late 15th century

Another new method of spanning a crossbow was the 'crow's foot' shown here; though sometimes used in war, it appears to have been more popular for hunting or target-shooting. This infantryman still has a deep sallet with a hinged nasal, but his armour is otherwise lighter than in earlier periods. The iron breastplate also has very early forms of tassets to protect his thighs. Otherwise the man's legs are only defended by light greaves. His sword, with the vertical guard, may again reflect Balkan or German influence. (Main sources: *St Ursula cycle* by Carpaccio 1493, Academia, Venice; *Attendants of Luigi Gonzaga*, wall painting by Domenico Morone 1496, Palazzo Ducale, Mantua; Venetian helmet from Khalkis, 15th C., Historical Mus., Athens.)

E2: Venetian militiaman of the Compagni della Calza, late 15th century

Handguns were increasingly important in the late 15th century. This example is a very simple form ignited with a separate heated iron *touche*. Apart from a light helmet with separate ear-pieces, this young man is unarmoured, though his extravagant costume is in the height of Venetian fashion and shows him to be a member of one of the 'Trouser

Clubs'. He also carries a broad-bladed *cinquadea* short-sword on his hip. (Main sources: *St Ursula cycle* by Carpaccio 1493, Academia, Venice; hand-gun, mid-15th C., Mus. Civico, Trieste.)

E3: Venetian man-at-arms, late 15th century

In complete contrast to the unarmoured hand-gunner, this man-at-arms is equipped for close combat with the three-pointed *ronco*, a peculiar weapon that proved very popular in Italy. His armour is a magnificent example of full plate 'white armour' made in northern Italy and exported throughout Europe. The arm defences are slightly different for each arm. His large iron sallet is of an almost fully enclosed type, having much in common with some ancient Greek helmets. (Main sources: *St Ursula cycle* by Carpaccio 1493, Academia, Venice; *Attendants of Luigi Gonzaga*, wall painting by Domenico Morone 1496, Palazzo Ducale, Mantua; Venetian helmet from Khalkis, 15th C., Historical Mus., Athens.)

F: The early 16th century

F1: 'Stradiot' light cavalryman from Dalmatia, c.1500

Stradioti were always lightly armoured or even unarmoured, but few illustrations survive showing those recruited in the southern and easternmost parts of the Venetian empire. This man probably comes from Dalmatia or Istria in what is now Yugoslavia. His bow is of the Asiatic composite type. His curved sabre is similar to those used in the Ottoman Empire, while his shield is of a typically eastern European or Hungarian form. His light armour is, however, typically Italian. (Main sources: *St Ursula cycle* by Carpaccio 1493, Academia, Venice; *Cavalcade*, wall painting 1474, church of St Mary, Beram, Istria.)

F2: Venetian light cavalryman, c.1500

Venetian domestic and Italian cavalry were divided into light and heavy units, though the main difference seems to have been in the use or otherwise of horse-armour. This man, as a light cavalryman, has a visored sallet instead of the closed armet used by heavy cavalry. His armour is also of a fluted variety; though made in northern Italy it could reflect the influence of German armourers, who made much greater use of fluting for both decoration and strengthening. (Main sources:

Unknown knight by Piero di Cosimo c.1515, Nat. Gallery, London; *St George* by Carpaccio c.1500, Scuola di S. Giorgio degle Sciavoni, Venice.)

F3: Greek nobleman from Venetian-ruled territory, early 16th century

The little that is known about aristocratic costume in 16th-century Greece shows it to have been strongly influenced by Ottoman Turkish styles. On the other hand, this man's short tunic is clearly European. His sword was made in Italy; and his brimmed hat was a style seen throughout the Balkans and Hungary. (Main sources: *St Ursula cycle* by Carpaccio 1493, Academia, Venice; *Adoration of the Magi* wall painting late 15th C., Mus. Civico, Padua.)

G: An assassination attempt in Venice around 1600

G1: Venetian 'Bravo', late 16th century

Venice was one of the main centres of Western fashion during the 16th century, and records indicate that hired bodyguards or thugs known as *Bravi* were among the most extravagantly dressed men in the city. This individual fights with a rapier and left-handed dagger in a characteristic late 16th century form of fencing. (Main sources: *Unknown Venetian nobleman* by Moroni, mid-16th C., Nat. Gallery, London; 'Venetian Bravo', in Vecellio's *Costume Book*, published 1589.)

G2: Escaped galley-slave, early 17th century

Venetian galley-slaves and those convicts who served their sentences at the oars wore similar costumes; this was totally inadequate for the rigours of life in an open war-galley and many died from exposure. The weapons that this man has seized include a long-hafted halbard, a dagger from Croatia, and a peculiar form of heavy matchlock pistol with a revolving triple barrel. (Main sources: 'Galley slave', in Vecellio's *Costume Book*; Venetian halberd, early 17th C., Armoury of Doge's Palace, Venice.)

G3: Venetian knight, c.1600

Most armours that survive in museums lack their original lining. This was often extended to form a decorative fringe around certain pieces, as shown here. This wealthy aristocrat has a helmet of the close helm form. His sword is very heavy compared to the rapier of his opponent. Iron shields were a relatively late development; although designed to withstand pistol and musket balls, they were probably more decorative than effective. (Main source: full armour, Milanese or Brescian *c.*1570, Mus. Civico Marzoli, Brescia.)

H: The death of Tommaso Morosini, 1647
H1: Tommaso Morosini, c.1647

By the mid-17th century the great age of armour had ended. A few full armours were worn by heavy cavalry and by commanding officers for prestige. At sea they would have been virtually suicidal, so here even Tommaso Morosini has been given a particularly fine form of half armour with a matching lobster-tail helmet. The broad nasal shows even more clearly the oriental inspiration of all such helmets. This particular suit of armour had two alternative types of protection for the hips and groin; the version worn here was for combat on foot, whereas the other was to be worn on horseback. Note that Morosini is armed with a basket-hilted rapier and a fine wheellock pistol. (Main source: mid-17th C. Brescian half armour, Mus. Civico Marzoli, Brescia.)

H2: Venetian arquebusier, early 17th century

The breastplate of this ordinary soldier has the same dent or 'proofing mark' as the fine armour of Tommaso Morosini. Though decorated, his breast and back plates, morion helmet and iron neck-protecting gorget worn beneath the breastplate are of much inferior quality. The man's sword is a Balkan *sciavona* while his arquebus has a German lock but was assembled at Brescia, in Venetian territory. (Main sources: 'Venetian infantryman', in Vecellio's *Costume Book*; Italian infantry armour, early 17th C., Armoury of the Palace of the Knights, Malta; sciavona sword, Venetian early 17th C., Armoury of the Doge's Palace, Venice.)

'Apotheosis of Admiral Lorenzo Marcello', victor of a naval battle in the Dardanelles in 1656 in which he himself died. Mid-17th century engraving. (Mus. Civ. Correr, Venice)

H3: 'Scappoli' galley volunteer, early 17th century

Unarmoured except for a small iron secrete helmet worn beneath his typical Balkan feathered cap, this volunteer is clearly from one of Venice's Balkan territories, probably northern Dalmatia. The decorative bands across his tunic had the same origin as the later decorations worn by hussar light cavalry. Apart from a simple dagger captured from the Ottomans, he is armed with a strange, all-iron combined war-axe and wheellock musket. (Main sources: 'Scappoli' in Vecellio's *Costume Book*; axe-gun, early 17th C., Armoury of the Doge's Palace, Venice.)

Notes sur les planches en couleur

A1 Le large bouclier de ce chevalier et le fait qu'il ne porte pas de surcot étaient courants en Italie au 13ème siècle. **A2** Les styles militaires dalmates étaient un mélange des modes balkanique et italienne; le bouclier de cet homme aurait été démodé en Europe occidentale, mais les boutons de sa tunique étaient très modernes. **A3** L'équipement de ce soldat est caractéristique de celui qui fut porté en Serbie médiévale ou dans l'Empire byzantin quoique l'épée soit occidentale.

B1 Bien équipé et armé par sa cité, cet arbalétrier porte un bouclier muni d'une pointe en fer à la base permettant de le ficher au sol lors des formations de 'remparts de bouclier'. **B2** La qualité de l'armure de ce soldat montre qu'il s'agit d'un mercenaire de l'armée professionnelle ou d'un chevalier; son javelot servait normalement lors des combats en mer. **B3** Chevalier armé selon le tout dernier style italien; ses jambarts sont en fer et le ventail de son casque est doublé au-dessus selon une mode propre à l'Italie.

C1 Jacopo Cavalli aurait normalement utilisé ce 'grand heaume', lourd, lors des parades; la plus grande partie de sa cotte de plates est cachée par un surcot qui se porte près du corps. **C2** La plus grande partie de l'armure de ce fantassin est faite en fer; il porte un bascinet italien caractéristique sur une coiffe de mailles désuète et une lance balkanique. **C3** Ce trompette ne porte pratiquement pas d'armure; son casque, avec pièce articulée couvrant les joues, pourrait avoir appartenu à un archer.

D1 Il existait au 15ème siècle plusieurs systèmes pour tendre des arbalètes plus puissantes—l'on voit ici un 'cranequin'. **D2** Notez le casque avec pièce de protection des joues à charnières et visière mobile. Le large bouclier est un style balkanique datant des siècles précédents. **D3** Bien que dalmate, ce chevalier italien, colonial, porte la meilleure armure italienne—notez les décorations en or sur son casque et la frange supplémentaire de mailles fixée au bas de sa cuirasse. **D4** Les simples arcs d'homme d'armes étaient considérés être des armes de paysans.

E1 Portant une armure plus légère qu'au cours des décennies précédentes, cet homme d'armes tend son arme avec un outil 'patte d'oie' (crow's foot). **E2** Ce soldat, habillé au goût de la meilleure mode vénitienne, mais portant seulement un casque en guise de protection, tire avec l'un des premiers pistolets. **E3** Contrairement à E2, cet homme est équipé pour le combat rapproché avec le ronco à trois pointes; sa salade est presque entièrement fermée.

F1 Portant une armure légère italienne, caractéristique, l'équipement de ce cavalier stradiot vient d'Europe orientale, ou, comme sa dague et son sabre de l'Empire ottoman. **F2** En tant que soldat de la cavalerie légère, ce personnage porte une salade à visière plutôt que l'armet fermé utilisé par la cavalerie lourde. **F3** Les aristocrates grecs du 16ème siècle furent profondément influencés par les modes turques, ottomanes, bien que la tunique courte de ce soldat soit visiblement européenne.

G1 Les bravi étaient des gardes du corps loués à Venise; cet homme combat avec un estoc et une dague pour gaucher selon un style d'escrime caractéristique. **G2** Cet esclave, échappé des galères, est pauvrement vêtu, mais il s'est emparé d'une variété d'armes y compris un mousquet à mèche, singulier, à triple canon révolver. **G3** Notez la frange décorative autour des pièces de l'armure de ce noble. Son bouclier était probablement plus décoratif qu'efficace.

H1 Tommaso Morosini porte une demi-armure splendide et un casque queue d'homard extrêmement lourd et dangereux en mer. **H2** Bien que la cuirasse de cet arquebusier porte la même 'marque de poinçon' que son armure, elle est de qualité inférieure. Son arquebuse a une platine allemande, mais fut assemblée à Brescia en territoire vénitien. **H3** Notez l'étrange combinaison de la hache de guerre avec le mousquet à platine à roulette; sa coiffure à plumes montre qu'il vient de Dalmatie.

Farbtafeln

A1 Das grosse Schild dieses Ritters und der fehlende Wappenrock bildeten die normale Ausrüstung im Italien des 13 Jahrhunderts. **A2** Die dalmatinischen Uniformen waren eine Mischung aus Stilrichtungen des Balkans und Italiens. Das Schild dieses Mannes wäre in Westeuropa bereits als veraltet angesehen worden; die Knöpfe an seinem Waffenrock waren jedoch sehr modern. **A3** Im Mittelalter wurde in Serbien, im byzantinischen Reich, diese Ausrüstung benutzt, obgleich das Schwert westlichem Ursprungs war.

B1 Ein Armbrustschütze, der durch seine Heimatstadt gut ausgerüstet wurde, hat ein Schild mit einer Eisenspitze, die man in den Erdboden rammte, wenn eine 'Schildwand' gebildet wurde. **B2** Die hohe Qualität dieser Ausrüstung lässt darauf schliessen, dass es sich um einen Berufssöldner oder einen Ritter handelte. Das Speer wurde bei Seeschlachten eingesetzt. **B3** Ein Ritter, der im neuesten italienischen Stil ausgerüstet ist. Die Beinschienen sind aus Eisen gefertigt, und sein Aventail ist doppelt gelegt, so wie es im italienischen Stil üblich war.

C1 Der schwere 'grosse Helm' von Jacopo Cavelli wurde gewöhnlich nur bei Paraden getragen; der Grossteil der Abzeichen wurde durch den enganliegenden Wappenrock verdeckt. **C2** Der Schutzpanzer dieses Infanteristen war vorwiegend aus Eisen hergestellt. Er trägt den typischen italienischen Bascinet über der altmodischen Kettenpanzerkappe und ist mit dem im Balkan üblichen Speer bewaffnet. **C3** Dieser Trompeter hat im Grunde überhaupt keinen Schutzpanzer. Der Helm—der wahrscheinlich einem Bogenschütze gehörte—hat ein Kinnstück, welches mit einem Scharnier versehen ist.

D1 Im 15. Jahrhunderten gab es bereits verschiedene Techniken einen kräftigeren Bogen in der Armbrust einzuspannen. Abgebildet ist ein Cranequin. **D2** Am Helm fallen besonders das mit Scharnieren versehene Kinnstück und das bewegliche Visier auf. Das grosse Schild ist im jahrhundertealten Balkanstil gehalten. **D3** Obwohl es sich um einen Dalmatier handelt, trägt dieser Ritter aus der italienischen Kolonialzeit die beste italienische Schutzpanzerung. Zu bemerken sind die goldenen Verzierungen am Helm und die zusätzlichen Kettenpanzerungen, die am unteren Ende der Brustplatten befestigt wurden. **D4** Die einfachen Langboden wurde als Bewaffnung der Bauern abgetan.

E1 Dieser Langbogenschütze trägt einen leichteren Schutzpanzer, als es zu Beginn des Jahrhunderts der Fall war. Er spannt seinen Bogen mit einem 'Krähenfuss'. **E2** Dieser Mann ist in der Bekleidung der Blütezeit des venezianischen Stils zu sehen. Er trägt lediglich einen Schutzhelm und schiesst mit einem frühen Handpistole. **E3** Nicht wie der Mann in E2 ist dieser für den Nahkampf mit einem dreizackigen Ronco ausgerüstet. Sein Sallet-Helm ist fast vollkommen geschlossen.

F1 Ein Stradiot Kavallerist mit dem typischen, leichten italienischen Schutzpanzer stammte aus Osteuropa oder wie sein Dolch und Säbel aus dem osmanischen Reich. **F2** Ein Mitglied der leichten Kavallerie hat hier einen Sallet-Helm mit Visier und nicht die geschlossene Sturmhaube, die von der schweren Kavallerie getragen wurde. **F3** Die griechischen Aristokratan des 16. Jahrhunderts wurden durch den türkisch-osmanischen Trend sehr beeinflusst, obgleich der kurze Waffenrock dieses Mannes ganz deutlich europäischem Ursprungs ist.

G1 Bravi hiessen die angeheuerten Leibwächter in Venedig; dieser Mann kämpft mit einem Rapier und in der linken Hand hält er einen Dolch, was bezeichnend für die Art des Fechtens war. **G2** Dieser Galeerensklave ist schlecht bekleidet, hat aber verschiedene Waffen erbeutet. Darunter befindet sich eine eigenartige Luntenschloss-Muskete mit einem drehbaren dreifachen Gewehrlauf. **G3** Auffallend ist der verzierte Besatz, der teilweise am Schutzpanzer dieses Edelmanns zu sehen ist. Sein Schild dient wohl eher der Zierde als der Verteidigung.

H1 Tommaso Morosine trägt hier eine wunderbare Halbpanzerung und einen Helm mit hummerähnlichem Endstück, der ziemlich schwer ist und auf See gefährlich ist. **H2** Obgleich die Brustplatten dieses Arkebusiers beschlagen und zisiliert sind, wie die in H1 abgebildet, zeugen sie nicht von der gleichen Qualitätsstufe. Sein Arkebuse hat ein deutsches Schloss, das aber in Brescia, auf venezianischem Gebiet, zusammengebaut wurde. **H3** Zu bemerken ist die eigentümliche Zusammenstellung von Kriegsbeil und Lenkschlossmuskete; seine mit Feder versehene Kappe deutet darauf hin, dass er aus Dalmatien stammt.